ABA
Visualized

*A visual guidebook
for parents and teachers*

Acknowledgements

We would first like to thank our amazingly talented illustrator, Saliha, who has assisted us with making these behavioral strategies come to life. With her help, we were able to capture details and emotions in the drawings so that readers can quickly grasp the concepts and relate to each image. We would also like to thank Anesa, who provided her unique perspective as a Behavior Analyst as well as a parent. Her involvement enabled our book to reach wide audiences, inclusive of every background. Thank you to Wynne and Igor for the detailed review of each integral part of the book so that we could be proud of our final product. We are also grateful for the many volunteers who tested our book and provided meaningful feedback. Finally, we would like to acknowledge our immensely supportive friends and family who have supported and encouraged us throughout this project.

First published 2019

ABA Visualized is a product of Studio van Diepen LLC

Written by:
Morgan van Diepen

Design and Art Direction by:
Boudewijn van Diepen

Illustrations/Infographics by:
Boudewijn van Diepen, Saliha Caliskan

Edited by:
Wynne Kemmeries, Igor Kana, Anesa Doyle

www.ABAvisualized.com
info@ABAvisualized.com

www.StudiovanDiepen.com
mail@StudiovanDiepen.com

ISBN: 978-0-578-47232-4

Printed by Lightning Source in a sustainable way

Contents

Note from the Authors

This book was created out of a desire to assist parents and teachers in learning effective strategies that will, in turn, improve their own children's and students' skills. While there are great behavior management resources available, our specific aim is to teach these strategies in a way that is easy to learn and easy to remember. By visualizing strategies that have been proven through research to be effective, we hope the concepts are now easily understandable and relatable to your individual needs. We hope this book gives you confidence as you practice each of the skills and support your child or student's growth.

Thank you,
Morgan and Boudewijn van Diepen

About the Authors

Morgan van Diepen

Morgan is a Board Certified Behavior Analyst (BCBA) with over ten years of working experience in the field of ABA. Starting as a 1:1 therapist in home and school settings, she quickly realized her passion for creating a positive impact on others' lives. With further experience and education, Morgan began training parents and teachers on how to use ABA strategies to best support their individual needs and improve their students' quality of life. Her research on using visuals to support parent learning (in particular, with non-native English speaking families), was presented at the internationally recognized ABAI conference in May 2019. Morgan continues to act as an advocate for approachable and accessible behavioral services for families and teachers.

Boudewijn van Diepen

Boudewijn is an award-winning infographic designer who approaches every project from a conceptual and original perspective. His ability to effectively shape complex information into an understandable and aesthetically attractive visual is evidenced through his more than seven years of diverse experience ranging from projects for government agencies to start-up nonprofit organizations. Boudewijn loves to use his creativity to make the world a more approachable place.

Our Mission

As an Applied Behavior Analysis (ABA) provider, I have had the opportunity to work with countless families and teachers over the years. I have heard a "nonverbal" child's first word, have helped an adult build his first friendship, and have seen individuals surpass goals of skills they were told they could never do. Each little step of progress makes an impact on not just the individual and their family, but also on me. Helping others to become more independent and more able to appropriately express themselves is tremendously rewarding. Our mission with ABA Visualized is to make effective ABA strategies accessible to everyone. We hope to support families and teachers as they teach essential skills and promote student independence. We aim to do this by teaching effective strategies in an easy to understand and easy to use format.

Research continues to show a direct link between parent involvement in skill development and outcome improvements. Through my own experience, I have also found this to be true. While individuals can make great gains through their ABA therapy sessions, the ones who make the most progress and sustain those skills over time are those who have parents who are actively involved in the teaching. As parent and teacher training have been determined to be a crucial component in the individual's progress, I searched for materials and teaching methods to most effectively involve parents and teachers. Most of what I found comprised of textual resources written with behavioral jargon or teaching methods involving verbally explaining and acting out strategies. I quickly realized challenges with these teaching methods: parents and teachers often do not have time to read lengthy explanations of how to use a strategy or may not have access to a behavioral expert to model and explain each strategy to them. These challenges became more apparent while working with families from various backgrounds who use English as a second language. Understanding lengthy texts or even verbal instructions on how to do a strategy became laborsome and on some occasions, led to the strategies being learned incorrectly. It was through these experiences that my husband and co-author proposed a new way of teaching: through visuals.

We hope that by visualizing ABA strategies, you are more easily able to understand and use them, and in turn, more effectively help the individuals in your life.

An Introduction

ABA

What is ABA?

Applied Behavior Analysis, or ABA, is a treatment approach that aims to improve the lives of individuals by a meaningful degree. The science of behavior analysis helps us to understand how behavior works, how behavior is affected by the environment, and how learning takes place. These findings are then applied to real-life situations in order to teach skills that will improve the individual's quality of life. The goal of ABA is to decrease behaviors that are harmful or impact learning while increasing behaviors that are helpful and meaningful to the individual.

Why is ABA effective?

ABA utilizes evidence-based strategies, meaning they have met rigorous criteria showing that they are useful, of high quality and effective. These strategies can be applied to daily life including home, school and community settings. Further, they have shown to be effective across the lifespan, starting from as young as two months old through adulthood.

A variety of skills can be taught using strategies based on the principles of ABA, including: social skills, language and communication, following directions, eye contact, learner readiness, self-care and adaptive skills, attending, motor skills, and self-regulation.

Who can use ABA?

Although ABA is often affiliated with individuals with Autism Spectrum Disorder, its concepts can be applied to any learner. In fact, ABA strategies have been used to effectively improve healthy eating habits, increase exercise patterns, learn a new language, improve accuracy in sports, train animals, and build workplace efficiency.

While ABA therapy is available to individuals with a diagnosis (e.g. Autism Spectrum Disorder, ADHD, OCD, Intellectual Disability, Down Syndrome, etc.), the strategies used during therapy have shown to be helpful to typical developing individuals as well. Further, anyone can learn how to implement these strategies: service providers, teachers, parents and other caretakers. Because the strategies are able to be adjusted per individual needs, ABA is accessible to all.

Autism & Other Disorders

Introduction

While principles of Applied Behavior Analysis can be found in a variety of professions and settings, the most well-known and commonly used application is its use with individuals with Autism. A major factor in linking ABA and Autism was an in-depth study completed by The National Professional Development Center (NPDC, 2014) which determined 27 specific ABA interventions as effective for individuals with Autism. A follow-up study by the National Standards Project (NSP, 2015) found substantial agreement. These comprehensive studies, in addition to many specialized studies, have resulted in the Center for Disease Control and Prevent (CDC) listing Behavior Therapy as an effective intervention for individuals with a range of disorders including, but not limited to: Attention Deficit Hyperactive Disorder (ADHD), Oppositional Defiant Disorder (ODD), Obsessive-Compulsive Disorder (OCD), Depression, Anxiety, Post Traumatic Stress Disorder (PTSD), and Autism Spectrum Disorder (ASD). In the following text, we have selected four of the disorders that are most commonly associated with ABA techniques to look at more in-depth.

For an individual to be diagnosed with a disorder, there must be a set of problems which result in significant difficulty, distress, and/or impairment in a person's life. However, ABA strategies can also be beneficial for individuals who do not have a specific disorder as the strategies to not target treating a disorder, but rather are a means of making meaningful behavior change.

Autism

Autism Spectrum Disorder (ASD) refers to a developmental diagnosis including notable challenges with social skills, speech and communication, and engagement in repetitive behaviors or focal interests. Individuals may present a wide range of abilities and challenges, leading to the understanding of Autism occurring on a spectrum. Some of the behaviors that are commonly present in individuals with ASD include: delayed learning of language, lack of eye contact, challenges with executive functioning (e.g. reasoning, planning, problem solving), narrow and intense interests, poor motor skills, sensory sensitivity, and engagement in problematic behaviors (e.g. tantrums, aggression, self-injury, elopement). During play, children with ASD may often focus on their restricted interests or repetitive behavior, thereby creating limited opportunities for peer interaction as well as the acquisition of appropriate play and social skills. Individuals with ASD often have a particular skill or interest that they tend to talk about and engage in. In some cases, this interest can be refined and harnessed in a way that leads to productive peer relationships and vocational skills.

Recent increased awareness and early diagnosis/intervention have led to increased prevalence rates (currently 1 in 59). Early diagnosis and intervention have led to early access to individualized services and supports which have shown to improve the individual's life significantly.

Causes of Autism

While there is not a proven cause of ASD, recent research indicates genetics as a significant contributing factor. A report by The Autism Society of America concluded that Autism has no racial, ethnic, or social boundaries and that family income, lifestyle, and education level do not affect the chance of Autism occurrence. In 2014, a comprehensive and influential research study evaluating the familial risk of Autism was published by Sandlin and his research team. Their results showed strong evidence for heritability and genetic influence in individuals with Autism. They determined the risk of an individual having a sibling with Autism was ten times greater than an individual with no sibling diagnosis. An individual with a cousin diagnosed with Autism would be two times more likely also to receive the diagnosis. Overall, Sandlin and his team estimated Autism hereditability to be 50%. In summary, the most accepted belief relating to the impact of genetics is that genes play an influential role in diagnosis of Autism, however it may not be an absolute role. Ongoing genetic research hopes to identify a clear biological cause which can impact prevention and treatment strategies.

Early signs of Autism

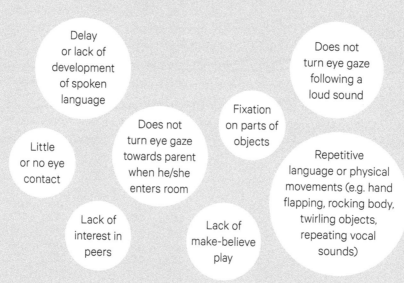

Delay or lack of development of spoken language

Does not turn eye gaze following a loud sound

Fixation on parts of objects

Little or no eye contact

Does not turn eye gaze towards parent when he/she enters room

Repetitive language or physical movements (e.g. hand flapping, rocking body, twirling objects, repeating vocal sounds)

Lack of interest in peers

Lack of make-believe play

Down Syndrome

Down Syndrome (DS), also known as Trisomy 21, is a condition in which a person is born with an extra chromosome (chromosome 21). Currently, Down Syndrome cannot be prevented, but it can be detected during pregnancy.

Although individuals with Down Syndrome may look similar, each person has different levels of abilities. Individuals often experience developmental delays; thus it is important to foster the development of strengths and talents in congruence with basic skills. Children with Down Syndrome may need assistance with self-care, including bathing, dressing and grooming.

The Centers for Disease Control and Prevention states the current rate of Down Syndrome as 1 in 700 births in the United States, making Down Syndrome the most common chromosomal disorder.

The physical features and medical problems associated with Down Syndrome vary child to child, but there are certain features that are commonly shared.

Early signs of Down Syndrome

Low muscle tone (hypotonia) and slower growth rate compared to typical peers

Flat facial profile with upward slant to the eyes, smaller than average size ears, and a protruding tongue

Increased risk for comorbid diseases (including congenital heart defect, pulmonary hypertension, and hearing and vision challenges)

Mild to moderate intellectual impairment

ADHD

Attention Deficit Hyperactivity Disorder (ADHD) is one of the most common neurodevelopmental disorders in childhood, occurring in 11% of children aged 4-17. Typically, children are diagnosed in their early school years due to trouble paying attention, controlling impulsive behaviors or being overly active. For individuals with ADHD, these problems are persistent and interfere with academic and social life. The key behaviors of ADHD are inattention and hyperactivity/impulsivity. People with ADHD might only face one of these problem behaviors, while others may have combined challenges.

While the specific cause of ADHD is unknown, current research shows that genetics plays an important role in its prevalence. Alternatively, research does not support the views that ADHD can be caused by a high-sugar diet, watching too much television, parenting styles, or environmental factors including family dynamic and poverty.

The symptoms of ADHD can change over time as a person ages; thus it is essential to teach specific skills that can reduce the challenges these individuals may face. For example, individuals could be taught specific strategies for organization and time management or behavioral strategies for reducing frequent fidgeting.

Common signs of ADHD

OCD

Obsessive-Compulsive Disorder (OCD) is an anxiety-related disorder in which individuals have recurring, unwanted thoughts, ideas or sensations (obsessions), that make them feel driven to do something repetitively (compulsions). In individuals with OCD, compelling behaviors take up a significant amount of time (more than one hour each day) and commonly interfere with other daily activities. Children often report that they do these behaviors in order to prevent something bad from happening or to 'make them feel better.'

OCD equally affects men, women and children of all races and socioeconomic backgrounds at a rate of about 1 in 100 children. Individuals with OCD may also experience anxiety, depression, or increased engagement in disruptive behaviors. The cause of OCD is unknown; however, current research is supporting genetic and hereditary factors.

Common themes of obsessions

Need for things to be in an orderly and symmetrical manner

Extreme thoughts of harming self or others

Unwanted and pervasive thoughts, including aggression or sexual urges

Fear of contamination

Common themes of compulsions

Following a strict routine

Checking

Washing and cleaning

Counting

Orderliness

Demanding repetitive reassurances

Book Overview

In the following chapters, you will learn how to use ABA strategies to improve your student's skill growth as well as reduce problematic behaviors. The strategies are organized by the following chapters:

- **Proactive Strategies:** strategies that can be used to prevent problem behavior from occurring and increase compliance
- **Reactive Strategies:** strategies that can be used to manage problem behavior and strengthen appropriate behavior
- **Teaching New Skills:** strategies that can be used to teach a variety of specific skills to the student
- **Putting it All Together:** step by step instructions for how to manage specific, common challenging situations
- **Tools:** blank templates and tools that you can use alongside the strategies.

Who can use

Although ABA strategies are typically implemented by ABA providers such as BCBA's and Behavior Therapists, these strategies can be successfully learned and used by parents, caregivers and teachers. In fact, we encourage these strategies to be used by all caretakers in the target individual's life. In each strategy, you will see the main characters being called "teacher" and "student" in order to encompass all types of individuals who will be teaching the skills and all ages of individuals who will be learning the skills.

Where to use

Some strategies featured are more salient in home settings and some are used primarily in school settings; however, the vast majority of strategies can be used at home, at school and in community settings. We encourage you to use these visual strategies wherever the most support is needed. You will have the most success if the strategies are consistently used across all settings.

How to use

This is your guidebook - use it in the way that helps you and your family the most! You may decide to read cover to cover then go back to strategies that were most relevant to you. Alternatively, you may choose to use the Flow Chart of Strategies (pg. 25) to identify a strategy that could support your current challenge or priority. Either way, once you are ready to try out a strategy, we suggest that you role-play or practice it first.

You can continue to use the visual as a guide until you feel confident you can complete the steps on your own. Each strategy can be used in a variety of situations, so it may help to refer back to the steps when you want to try an alteration.

In addition to the individual strategies, there are suggested steps to managing common challenges (pg. 109), in which you can use several strategies together to tackle a more difficult situation.

Lastly, in the back of the book, you will find a "Tools" section in which there are templates for you to cut out or make a copy and use to support some of the strategies you have learned about.

What to expect

The strategies featured in the following chapters have all shown to be effective; however, individuals may experience success at different rates. As behavior is developed from a pattern of experiences, it is important to remember that behavior change does not often occur immediately. The best way to utilize the strategies to create impactful behavior change and see results is to be consistent. For example, if you are using a proactive strategy to increase compliance with challenging demands (e.g. Priming; First, Then), use that strategy every time you give a demand. Additionally, teach other family members and teachers to use the same strategy when giving demands. This consistency will most effectively change the student's behavior. In short, be persistent and patient!

In regards to reducing problematic behavior, you will learn a very effective strategy called extinction. To give a brief introduction, extinction is when you first learn why a student is engaging in a problematic behavior and then you stop providing access to whatever is maintaining that behavior. When using this strategy, you should expect that an extinction burst may occur. An extinction burst in simple terms means "it may get worse before it gets better." If an extinction burst is occurring and problematic behaviors are getting worse (increasing amount of occurrences or increasing in intensity), it means you are doing the strategy correctly and you must continue being consistent. The student is learning that what used to work (e.g. yelling used to lead to gaining parent attention), is no longer working, due to your use of extinction. Some students may try other ways of obtaining what they want (e.g. yelling louder, yelling and crying, etc.), thus, creating an extinction burst. An effective way of reducing the likeness of experience this burst is to simultaneously use the Teaching Better Behaviors strategy in order to teach the student the appropriate way of getting their needs met. Use this strategy in alignment with extinction for best results.

Strategies Overview

In order to guide you through choosing which strategy will best suit your individual situation, we have created a flow chart of all the featured strategies. Find your personal goal on the left side of the chart, then follow the lines to identify which strategies may be effective at reaching this goal. It is important to note that multiple strategies may be beneficial and we encourage you to try them all to see which combination leads to positive results for you. Remember that consistency is key, so when you choose a strategy to practice, continue to use it daily!

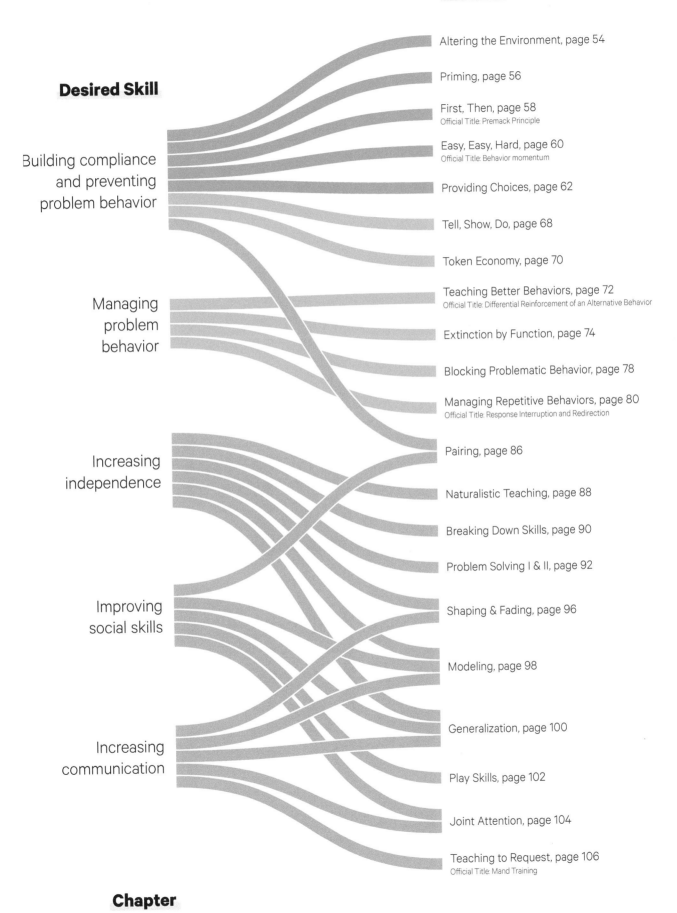

Strategy

Desired Skill

Building compliance and preventing problem behavior

Managing problem behavior

Increasing independence

Improving social skills

Increasing communication

Altering the Environment, page 54

Priming, page 56

First, Then, page 58
Official Title: Premack Principle

Easy, Easy, Hard, page 60
Official Title: Behavior momentum

Providing Choices, page 62

Tell, Show, Do, page 68

Token Economy, page 70

Teaching Better Behaviors, page 72
Official Title: Differential Reinforcement of an Alternative Behavior

Extinction by Function, page 74

Blocking Problematic Behavior, page 78

Managing Repetitive Behaviors, page 80
Official Title: Response Interruption and Redirection

Pairing, page 86

Naturalistic Teaching, page 88

Breaking Down Skills, page 90

Problem Solving I & II, page 92

Shaping & Fading, page 96

Modeling, page 98

Generalization, page 100

Play Skills, page 102

Joint Attention, page 104

Teaching to Request, page 106
Official Title: Mand Training

Chapter

● Proactive Strategies   ● Reactive Strategies   ● Teaching New Skills

Foundations of ABA

Introduction

ABA was founded on several core principles that remain the core of the field today. These principles guide decision making in which strategies should be used, how to best use them, and how to determine if they are effective.

Focus on observable behavior

ABA focuses on the observable aspects of behavior, meaning what we can see happening. We pay attention to what events occurred before and after the behavior to provide us clues as to why the behavior is occurring. It is believed that by assessing the environment and factors surrounding a behavior, we can begin to understand why the behavior is taking place; thus we can begin to change it. In ABA, we look for reasons in the environment to explain why an individual engages in a behavior, rather than explaining the behavior through their feelings, mood, or even their diagnosis.

Being objective

An essential part of practicing ABA is being objective. This starts from the beginning when we are first describing the behavior we want to change or the skill we want to teach. The word 'tantrum' likely creates a different image in different people's minds. Do you imagine the individual crying, screaming, laying on the ground, running away, saying 'no,' or any other behaviors? These are all observable and specific behaviors that we want to use when describing a goal to 'reduce tantrums.' You will learn how to describe a behavior in objective terms so that you can accurately track the progress of changing this behavior over time. Once you have created a clear description of the behavior you would like to change, you will learn how to collect data so you can determine if the strategies you are using are helping. The process of collecting data and assessing results is the objectiveness that makes ABA so effective. If the data shows we are not making progress towards our goal, we are able to recognize this and change approaches.

Ways of describing a behavior

Crying
Knees on ground
Hands in hair
Yelling

Upset
Angry
Having a bad day
Meltdown

Individualized

A final factor of what makes ABA unique is that the strategies can be adapted to meet the needs of each individual. On each visual strategy, you will see the action steps and an example of a situation in which the strategy could be used. We encourage you to use the strategies in the situations that are most meaningful to you. For example, in teaching the skill of requesting items (pg. 106), the individual may be expected to make a four-word request ("I want play outside"), a one-word request ("outside"), the ASL sign for 'outside,' or use a picture exchange system to hand a picture of 'outside' to another person. The steps of the strategy remain the same, however, the expectations may be altered to fit the learner's skill level.

ABC of behavior

The ABCs of Behavior is a way to determine why a behavior is happening. In ABA, the term 'behavior' refers to any observable action that a person can do. This encompasses not only problematic behaviors, but also appropriate behaviors.

For many individuals with Autism or other related disorders, there may be problem behavior(s) that caretakers would like to reduce. The first step in behavior reduction is understanding why the behavior occurs. To do this, you will need to attend to what is happening before (antecedent) and after (consequence) the behavior. These are the two clues that will help you determine the reason (function) the behavior is occurring.

A   B   C

Antecedent
Events that occur immediately before a behavior

Behavior
An observable action

Consequence
Events that occur immediately after a behavior

ABC at home example
- Antecedent: Mother tells child get her shoes
- Behavior: Child screams
- Consequence: Mother gets the shoes herself

ABC at school example
- Antecedent: Teacher asks students a question
- Behavior: Student raises hand
- Consequence: Teacher calls on student

Instructions for filling out ABC Chart

1. Choose one behavior to target (e.g. tantrums, yelling, protest/saying 'no,' aggression, hand flapping, etc.).
2. Every time this behavior occurs, fill out the chart with (A) what happened immediately prior, (B) what the behavior looked like, (C) what happened immediately afterward. Optional: Add comments with more information about what was happening at that time (e.g. in the store, in the car, during bedtime routine, did/did not take medication this day).
3. Record information for at least four times the behavior occurs (can all be during one day if the behavior occurs a lot, or can be over several days if the behavior does not occur as often).

ABC Chart

Tantrum: Yelling, crying, falling to the ground

Antecedent What happened before the behavior?	Behavior Describe the behavior	Consequence What happened after the behavior?	Function
Mom told son to "turn off iPad"	yelled "no, no, no," and cried for 2 minutes	Mom took iPad	
Son asked Mom, "can I watch cartoons?" + Mom said "not right now."	Fell on ground, yelled "I want cartoons!" cried for 3 minutes	Mom told son to stop yelling	
Son was watching Super Wings with family	Yelled "I want Mickey Mouse!" fell to ground	Mom changed channel to Mickey Mouse	
Son asked Mom to buy chocolate cereal, Mom said "no"	Fell on ground, cried for 1 minute	Mom picked up son and put in shopping cart	

Practice

Choose a specific behavior to target. Describe that behavior using observable and objective words ("Target Behavior"). Fill out the chart below for the next four times that behavior occurs.

Note: Sometimes, a consequence is also the antecedent for the next behavior.
Example: (A) Instruction to do homework (B) student yells (C) teacher repeats the instruction to do homework // (A) teacher repeats the instruction to do homework (B) student rips paper (C) teacher tapes paper and repeats the instruction

ABC Chart

Target Behavior: _____

Antecedent	Behavior	Consequence	Function
What happened before the behavior?	Describe the behavior	What happened after the behavior?	

More Practice

Choose a specific behavior to target. Describe that behavior using observable and objective words ("Target Behavior"). Fill out the chart below for the next four times that behavior occurs.

ABC Chart

Target Behavior:

Antecedent	Behavior	Consequence	Function
What happened before the behavior?	Describe the behavior	What happened after the behavior?	

Functions of Behavior

Functions of behavior refers to the reason someone is engaging in a behavior. Understanding the 'why' is essential to aim to change that behavior. If an individual disrupts the classroom by frequently getting out of their seat to pace around the room, before we decide how to manage that behavior, we need to know why it is occurring. This initial understanding will lead to more success in the behavior management. In the field of Behavioral Analysis, it is believed that there are four functions, or reasons, that behavior may occur.

1. Attention (from others)
2. Access (to an item or activity)
3. Escape (from a demand)
4. Sensory (a feel-good sensation)

This means that for any behavior that is occurring, it is happening because the individual is either receiving attention, gaining access to an item/activity, escaping a demand or because it makes the individual feel good.

In the previous example about a student who paces around the classroom, we will need to determine: Is he gaining attention from the teacher/peers? Is he walking around the room in order to access some preferred items? Is the walking delaying or preventing him from completing an assigned task? Or is it fulfilling a sensory need for movement?

We can determine the function of the behavior by looking at the ABC's (pg 30). Use the ABC template (pg. 31) to record at least five occurrences of the problem behavior and the ABC's surrounding that behavior. With this information, we can look for patterns to choose which function is the reason for the behavior.

In the next examples, we will examine how one behavior could occur for four different reasons and how to determine the cause. The example behavior shown is a student engaging in self-injurious behavior (SIB) by hitting himself on the head.

Clues the behavior is Attention function

- The individual was previously receiving attention from someone then that person stopped giving attention just before the problem behavior occurred.
- Immediately after the problematic behavior, someone gave the individual attention. Remember that reprimands (e.g. "no," "don't do that") are also a form of attention.

The student receives attention after he engages in the behavior.

Here, following the SIB, the teacher is giving attention by comforting the student. Remember, reprimands ("don't do that," "stop," "no") are also forms of giving attention.

Clues the behavior is Access function

A preferred item or activity was taken away from the individual just before the problematic behavior occurred.

- The individual was told "no," "not right now" or "wait."
- Immediately after the problematic behavior, someone gave the individual a preferred item or activity.

The student engages in problematic behavior after being told "no," "not right now" or "wait."

Here, the student asked for the phone and was told "no" immediately prior to the SIB.

Clues that the behavior is Escape function

- The individual was instructed to complete a task just before the problem behavior occurred.
- Immediately after the problematic behavior, the expectation to complete a task was removed.

Following the problem behavior, the student is able to escape from a non-preferred task.

Here, following the SIB, the teacher is allowing the student to escape his work task by going to a quiet area to "calm down."

Clues that the behavior is Sensory function

- The behavior occurred when the individual was alone and no tasks were given.
- The behavior occurs across all people, settings, and activities.

The student is engaging in the behavior because it "feels good."

When the function is sensory, the student does not need the teacher in order to have reinforcement.

Once you are able to identify the function of the behavior, you are ready to move on to learning strategies that reduce this problematic behavior (pg. 39).

Instructions for choosing the function

Next, you will use the information you collected in columns A, B, and C as clues to make the best guess at which of the four functions is the reason the behavior is happening. You can circle the most important clue from each row to help guide your decision.

ABC Chart

Target Behavior: Tantrum: Yelling, crying, and falling to the ground

Antecedent What happened before the behavior?	Behavior Describe the behavior	Consequence What happened after the behavior?	Function
Mom told son to "turn off iPad"	yelled "no, no, no" and cried for 2 minutes	Mom took iPad	Access (iPad)
Son asked Mom, "can I watch cartoons?" + Mom said "not right now."	Fell to ground, yelled "I want cartoons!" cried for 3 minutes	Mom told son to stop yelling	Access (watching cartoons)
Son was watching Super Wings with family	Yelled "I want Mickey Mouse!" fell to ground	Mom changed channel to Mickey Mouse	Access (watching Mickey Mouse)
Son asked Mom to buy chocolate cereal, Mom said "no"	Fell to ground, cried for 1 minute	Mom picked up son and put in shopping cart	Access (chocolate cereal)

Function: Access

Practice

Fill out the chart below for the next four times the target behavior occurs. Look for clues to what is happening before or after the behavior. Use these clues to determine the function for each time the behavior occurred. On the line at the bottom, write the function that occurred most often.

ABC Chart

Target Behavior: _____

Antecedent	Behavior	Consequence	Function
What happened before the behavior?	Describe the behavior	What happened after the behavior?	

Function: _____

Alternative option: ABC Checklist

Instructions for filling out ABC Checklist: Fill this out every time you see the problematic behavior occur by checking off the boxes that relate to the particular incident. This may help you to identify if any trends are occurring or observe why the behavior is happening.

ABC Chart

Target Behavior: _____

Antecedent What happened before the behavior?	**Behavior** Describe the behavior	**Consequence** What happened after the behavior?	**Function**
☐ Was told "no" ☐ Was asked to do something ☐ Attention given to others ☐ Transition ☐ Nothing "out of the blue"	☐ Cries ☐ Hits ☐ Screams ☐ Throws object ☐ -------------	☐ Redirect to alternative behavior ☐ Told no ☐ Given what s/he wants ☐ Ignored ☐ Verbal reprimand	☐ Attention ☐ Access ☐ Escape ☐ Sensory
☐ Was told "no" ☐ Was asked to do something ☐ Attention given to others ☐ Transition ☐ Nothing "out of the blue"	☐ Cries ☐ Hits ☐ Screams ☐ Throws object ☐ -------------	☐ Redirect to alternative behavior ☐ Told no ☐ Given what s/he wants ☐ Ignored ☐ Verbal reprimand	☐ Attention ☐ Access ☐ Escape ☐ Sensory
☐ Was told "no" ☐ Was asked to do something ☐ Attention given to others ☐ Transition ☐ Nothing "out of the blue"	☐ Cries ☐ Hits ☐ Screams ☐ Throws object ☐ -------------	☐ Redirect to alternative behavior ☐ Told no ☐ Given what s/he wants ☐ Ignored ☐ Verbal reprimand	☐ Attention ☐ Access ☐ Escape ☐ Sensory

Function: _____

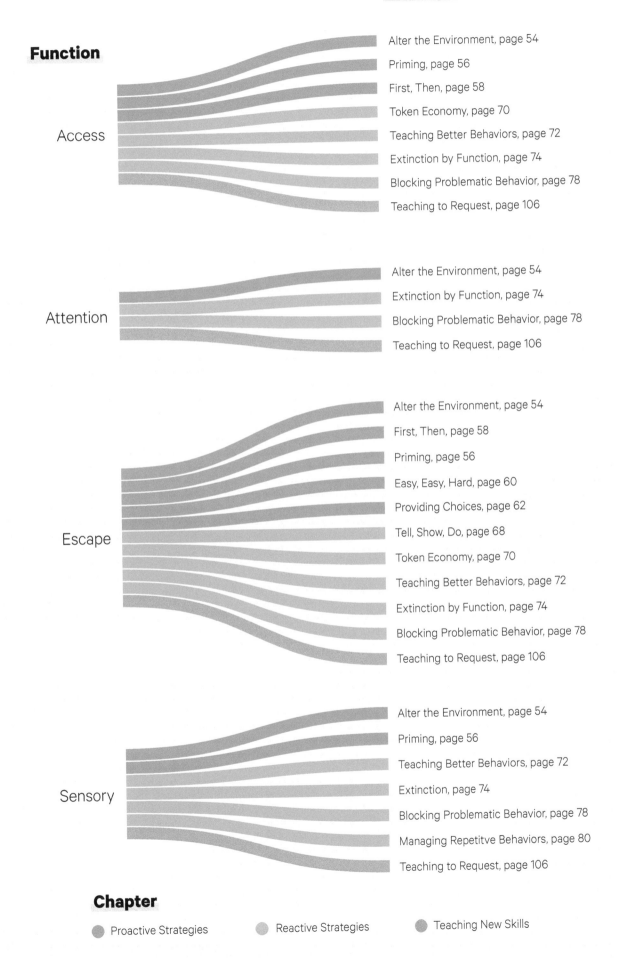

Function

Strategy

Access
- Alter the Environment, page 54
- Priming, page 56
- First, Then, page 58
- Token Economy, page 70
- Teaching Better Behaviors, page 72
- Extinction by Function, page 74
- Blocking Problematic Behavior, page 78
- Teaching to Request, page 106

Attention
- Alter the Environment, page 54
- Extinction by Function, page 74
- Blocking Problematic Behavior, page 78
- Teaching to Request, page 106

Escape
- Alter the Environment, page 54
- First, Then, page 58
- Priming, page 56
- Easy, Easy, Hard, page 60
- Providing Choices, page 62
- Tell, Show, Do, page 68
- Token Economy, page 70
- Teaching Better Behaviors, page 72
- Extinction by Function, page 74
- Blocking Problematic Behavior, page 78
- Teaching to Request, page 106

Sensory
- Alter the Environment, page 54
- Priming, page 56
- Teaching Better Behaviors, page 72
- Extinction, page 74
- Blocking Problematic Behavior, page 78
- Managing Repetitve Behaviors, page 80
- Teaching to Request, page 106

Chapter

● Proactive Strategies   ● Reactive Strategies   ● Teaching New Skills

Reinforcement/Punishment

In Behavior Analysis, reinforcement and punishment are understood as the underlying factors that influence all of our behavior. This is built on B.F. Skinner's research on behavior which determined that behavior can be taught or changed by controlling the consequences surrounding the action.

In short, reinforcement is something that makes the behavior likely to occur more in the future and punishment is something that makes the behavior likely to occur less in the future. It is important that we understand whether our responses to an individual's behavior are reinforcing (increasing) or punishing (decreasing) that behavior.

Example part 1
A student is talking out in class during math. The teacher sends the student to the hallway. The student liked being in the hallway because he didn't have to do math. In the future, he will talk out during math again (his behavior was increased, or reinforced).

Example part 2
A student is talking out in class during math. The teacher sends the student to the hallway. The student became embarrassed that he had to leave the class in front of his friends. In the future, he will not talk out during math (his behavior was decreased, or punished).

By understanding which responses will increase or decrease a behavior, we are then able to manipulate our responses in order to control that behavior. If we learn that receiving praise is reinforcing for an individual, we can give praise after he completes a task and expect that he will likely try that task again in the future. Alternatively, if we know that taking away electronics is punishing for an individual, we can take away electronics after he engages in a problematic behavior and expect that he will be less likely to engage in that problematic behavior in the future.

Although reinforcement and punishment are both impactful on changing behavior, in ABA, we heavily focus on reinforcement and only utilize punishment when reinforcement is not showing success. There are negative side effects with using punishment, but most importantly, punishment only aims to decrease a behavior. It does not teach the individual what behaviors they should do instead. In ABA, we prioritize reinforcing behaviors we want to see more and use extinction (pg. 74, 76) to stop reinforcing behaviors we want to see less.

Types of reinforcement

To look more in-depth at how reinforcement works, we must first understand the two types: positive reinforcement and negative reinforcement.

Positive reinforcement

Positive reinforcement simply means something is given, which makes the behavior more likely to occur in the future.

Common types of positive reinforcement

- Giving praise, compliments
- Giving high fives, tickles, smiling at the person
- Giving money
- Giving access to toys/electronics
- Giving preferred foods

Example: You do the dishes before your partner comes home from work. When your partner sees the clean dishes, he gives you a kiss and says 'thank you.' In the future, when you are home before your partner, you will be more likely to do the dishes. (The partner <u>gave</u> a kiss and praise, so this is <u>positive</u> reinforcement).

By giving something preferred (e.g. praise, stickers, tickles, preferred toys/food, etc.) following a behavior, that behavior will be more likely to occur in the future.

Here, the teacher is giving praise and a sticker following the student's on task behavior. He is likely to be on task again in the future to earn the praise and the sticker.

Negative reinforcement

Negative reinforcement means something is taken away, which makes the behavior more likely to occur in the future.

Common types of negative reinforcement

- Removing aversive noises
- Removing pain
- Removing annoying situations
- Removing aversive tasks

Example: You have a headache, so you take pain medicine. Shortly afterward, the headache pain is gone. In the future, when you have a headache, you will be more likely to take the pain medicine again. (The medicine <u>took away</u> the pain, so this is negative reinforcement).

By removing something non-preferred (e.g. a work task, non-preferred food, pain, aversive situation, etc.) following a behavior, that behavior will be more likely to occur in the future.

Here, the teacher is removing the work task following the student's on-task behavior, giving him "a break" from the task. He is likely to be on-task again in the future to earn another break from the task.

As these are both still reinforcement, the behavior will be more likely to occur in the future, whether something was taken away or added.

What's the difference between negative reinforcement and punishment?

To be "reinforcement," we know that the behavior will be more likely to occur in the future. Remember that the "negative" indicates that something was taken away, rather than the common understanding that negative = bad. Thus, negative reinforcement means that following a behavior, something was taken away, which will make that behavior more likely to occur in the future. Punishment rather, indicates that a behavior will be less likely to occur in the future.

Tips for using reinforcement

Reinforcement shapes how we behave, and for this reason, is the core of all ABA strategies. There are several factors which make reinforcement even more effective by leading to faster and/or more sustaining desired change.

Reinforcers should be personalized and preferred

Observe the student's interest and motivation in order to determine what reinforcer to use. To do this, set out a variety of items and activities that the student may like. Look to see which items engage his attention and the order in which he chooses the items. You can deduce that the item he chose first will be the most reinforcing, meaning, he will be more likely to work for that item.

Place a few preferred items around the room and watch which items naturally draws the student's attention. This is a quick and easy way to determine what is reinforcing in that moment.

Reinforcement should be immediate

In order for the student to learn what he's done is correct, the reinforcement should immediately follow the behavior. It is less likely that you will see the behavior increase if you give a delayed reinforcement. For example, if a student appropriately requests for play-doh, but you give the play-doh 15 minutes later, it is unlikely that he will associate his request with earning the play-doh.

Great, now you can play outside

First, decide what is most reinforcing for the student. Is it: praise, a break from a task, playing with an item/activity, earning a tangible reward?

When the student begins complying with a challenging task, give praise. When the student finishes the task, immediately give the student what is most valuable to them.

Amount of reinforcement should be matched to the behavior

Consider the difficulty of the task when deciding how much reinforcement to give.
The size of the reinforcer needs to fit the size of the effort. For example, if you have to provide a lot of assistance for the student to put on his shoes, you may give a little praise at the end (e.g. 'nice job pulling tight'), however, if the student ties his shoes on his own, you will want to give a lot of praise and possibly an extra reinforcer (e.g. a toy, favorite snack, etc.). In summary, save the big reinforcers and big excitements for harder tasks.

Nice trying

The more effort the student puts in, the more reinforcement he should get. Here, the teacher needed to support the student a lot with tying his shoes, so she gave a little praise.

If he did a new step of tying shoes for the first time on his own, she should show a lot more excitement (e.g. high fives, cheers, etc.).

Provide choices of reinforcers

Before giving a difficult demand, ask the student what they would like to work for. For many learners, it's beneficial to physically show two or three choices of activities/items that can be earned. Remember to follow through with giving that item immediately when the student finishes the task.

Prior to giving a demand, provide 2-3 choices of activities/items than can be earned. Use the specific item chosen as the reinforcer to motivate the student to complete the demand.

*see page 62 for more information on providing choices.

Limit access to reinforcers

Put away preferred items so they will maintain their effectiveness as reinforcers. If students have access all the time to their favorite toys, activities and food, they will be less motivated to work for these items. This may include physically putting away preferred items or limiting time on electronics. Rotate the items so that the student will maintain interest in a variety of items and activities and stay motivated to work for them.

Place preferred items in boxes or on a shelf that is out of reach. Limit access to these items in order to increase their effectiveness.

A student who has limited access to a favorite toy will be more motivated to work to earn it compared to a student who has free access to this toy throughout the day.

Fade reinforcement when skill is learned

When the student is learning a new skill, you should give reinforcement for every attempt. As the student begins to improve and do more of the skill independently, continue to reinforce their progress. When the student has learned to do the skill completely on their own, you can start to minimize the amount of reinforcement you are giving. For example, if a student is learning to put on his shirt, you may initially give praise for allowing you to help him, then for trying on his own, then finally, for doing it on his own. After a few days of him putting his shirt on by himself, you don't need to continue to praise every time.

For new skills: give praise and reinforcement for every attempt and every step in progressing towards independence. Once the student has learned to do the skill on their own: fade out the amount of praise and reinforcement you are giving. You can go from big cheers to 'nice job!' to thumbs up/high five. For independent skills: give praise randomly, only every few times the skill is complete.

Notes

Proactive Strategies

Introduction

Proactive strategies are tools used to <u>prevent</u> challenging behaviors from occurring. They are used before any challenging behaviors to help reduce the chances of them occurring. Most of us use proactive strategies in our daily lives to prevent frustration, disorganization, and overwhelming workloads. We actively create ways to stay organized and simplify our lives (e.g. To-Do lists, use of daily/weekly planners, take breaks throughout the workday, etc.). Individuals with Autism and other developmental disorders may need support in learning how to manage frustrating situations and how to better prepare for them.

The proactive strategies in the following chapter are effective in improving social, communication, behavior, play, school-readiness, academic, motor, and adaptive skills.

Goals
- Clarify student expectations
- Promote positive behaviors
- Prevent problematic behaviors
- Promote independence in self-management

Things to consider
- What types of instructions does the student best respond to? (e.g. 1-step, 2-step, visuals, etc.)
- Does the student do better with verbal reminders or visual supports?
- Does the student do better with a transition warning (Priming)?
- Can the student make choices when given two options (Providing Choices)?
- Does the student like social praise and attention?
- What appropriate behaviors does the student already do that could be focused on/rewarded more?
- Can the physical environment be changed to reduce problematic behavior? (Altering the Environment)
- Can I increase motivation through the use of student's interests? (First, Then)
- When giving instructions, do I answer all the following questions:

☐ What do I do?
☐ How much do I do?
☐ When is it finished?
☐ What do I do next?

For each problematic behavior you want to prevent from occurring, determine the function of that behavior (pg. 33). Consider, what are the usual 'triggers' for the behavior? Some triggers may not be preventable, but their impact could be lessened. Use the proactive strategies listed by function as ways to reduce the likelihood of the problematic behavior occurring.

How to use
- Determine the function of behavior
- Determine which strategy to try (based on the function)
- Know which situations to apply which strategy
- Be consistent in applying the strategies
- Reward the student as often as possible

Proactive strategies by function

Once you have determined the function of the target behavior, select a strategy from those listed below to practice. You may choose more than one strategy to use at a time, just make sure to be consistent in your use. It is important to note that one single use may or may not prevent the problematic behavior from occurring, but with repeated practice, you are more likely to see a change in the student's behavior.

Visual strategies for Attention
- In the classroom, move the student's seat closer to the teacher or to be facing away from other students (Altering the Environment, pg. 54)

Additional tips for Attention
- Teach appropriate ways to ask for help or initiate interactions with others
- Give attention more frequently when the student is not engaging in problematic behaviors ('catch them being good')

Visual strategies for Escape
- Provide choices relating to the task (Providing Choices, pg. 62)
- Use of visual supports that show expectations (e.g. "First, Then" tool, "Visual Schedule" tool, pg. 145, 140)
- Start with easier tasks and build up to the more challenging task (Easy, Easy, Hard, pg. 60)
- Inform of an upcoming task and expectations (Priming, pg. 56)

Additional tips for Escape

- Give clear and simple instructions
- Give breaks from the task more frequently when the student is not engaging in problematic behaviors ('catch them being good')
- Adjust the difficulty or length of the task
- Use schedules and timers
- Teach appropriate ways to ask for a break from a task or request for more time with a task

Visual strategies for Access

- Inform the student of an upcoming transition away from preferred items/ activities (Priming, pg. 56)
- Use of visual supports that show when the student can access the preferred item/ activity (e.g. "First, Then" tool, "Visual Schedule" tool, pg. 145, 140)

Additional tips for Access

Give access to preferred items more frequently when the student is not engaging in problematic behaviors ('catch them being good')

- Use of schedules and timers
- Teach appropriate ways to ask for items, activities and people

Visual strategies for Sensory

- Teach an alternative behavior they can do that will meet the same sensory need and provide easy access to that replacement activity (e.g. place exercise bands on the legs of a chair for the student to kick/bounce against instead of walking around the classroom) (Altering the Environment, pg. 54)

Additional tips for Sensory

- Teach how to find and use appropriate sensory items/activities independently

Altering the Environment

Changing the setting to set up the student for success

Goal

Plan ahead to prevent problematic behaviors from occurring

How

Identify elements that are likely triggers for problematic behavior. Consider how to limit those elements. Set up the environment to have limited triggers so the student is more likely to succeed.

Context

Consider the context in which the student typically engages in problematic behavior, then alter that environment to set the student up for success.

Examples

- Change where the student is sitting - minimize distraction
- Clear the table prior to starting homework to prevent throwing behavior
- Sitting between student and peer to prevent/block aggressive behavior

Tip

You can also alter the environment to promote positive behaviors. Try:

- Placing sensory items (see Recommended Products, pg. 150) where the student has easy access in order to promote appropriate sensory play
- Placing communication cards (see Tools, pg. 144) near the student while he is working on a difficult task as a reminder for how to ask for help

At school

Alter the environment

By creating a clear workspace, the student is more likely to attend to the task.

No alteration

When the workspace has items not necessary for the task, the student is more likely to be distracted.

In the community

Identify trigger

Recognize events or settings that may be a trigger for problematic behavior.
For this student, a peer approaching his toys is likely to lead to aggressive behavior.

Alter the environment

By intentionally changing the environment, the teacher is able to proactively plan for and prevent the problematic behavior. Here, the teacher sat close to the student and can encourage appropriate play with the peer.

No alteration

If no alteration is made, the problematic behavior is still likely to occur. Here, the teacher sat at a distance and the student was able to engage in aggressive behaviors when the peer approached him.

Priming

Preparing students in advance to increase their chance of success

Goal

Increase the student's success with an upcoming activity or event by preparing them for it in advance

How

Prior to a situation that may be difficult for the student, the teacher will inform the student about what is upcoming.

This can be through the use of a time countdown ("Five minutes until bedtime"), a verbal reminder of expectations prior to a new situation ("we're going to a birthday party tomorrow, remember we will sit and watch Kate open her presents"). Priming can be used in the classroom by showing the student the materials and modeling what to do prior to asking them to complete a new task.

Context

Use priming prior to situations that are often difficult for the student.

- transitions
- changes in schedule
- new situations
- starting a task

Tip

Try using a visual schedule (see "Tools" pg. 140) to prime the student for what will happen that day.

No prime, less success

By immediately presenting the difficult event (turning off electronics), the student may have little success with complying.

An upcoming event

Teacher will recognize that an upcoming event may be difficult for the student.

After prime, more success

Following the prime, the student is more likely to have success during the stressful event, as he was prepared for what was coming.

Give prime (immediately prior)

Remind the student of the upcoming expectation just prior to the possible difficult event.

Give prime (in advance)

Give student a prime in advance: either five minutes before a transition, or the day before a new event.

Official title: Premack Principle

First, Then

Using a simple statement
to increase compliance

Goal

Increase motivation and compliance in completing
tasks

How

Identify a reward that will likely be motivating for the
student (e.g. time on electronics, favorite snack, tickles).
Make a statement in the form: "first (target task), then
(reward)." Only give the reward once the student has
completed the target task.

Context

This easy to use phrase can be inserted throughout
the day in a variety of settings. Before giving a demand,
think if you can re-word it using a "first, then" phrase.

Tip

Use specific and simple language. For example,
instead of using words like "work hard," say the specific
expectation (e.g. "finish five problems,"
"sit quietly at your desk," "read for ten minutes").

Use this tip when describing the reward too (e.g. "five
minutes with whiteboard," "sit in beanbag chair during
story time").

Try using a visual "first, then" board to remind students
what they need to do in order to earn their reward (see
"Tools," pg. 145).

1

First do your homework.
Then you can watch tv

State demand using "first, then"

State the target task followed by the
reward that the student will earn. Choose a
reward that will likely be motivating to them.

Follow through

Follow through with the demand by restating the "first, then" phrase until the student has started complying. Remember to praise for starting the task!

Reinforcement

Following the completion of the task, remember to immediately provide the student with the reward that was promised.

Easy, Easy, Hard

Using a pattern of requests to increase compliance

Goal

Student will comply with a difficult target task (e.g. 'pick up your toys,' 'get on school bus,' 'complete ten math problems')

How

Increase the student's motivation and build compliance by starting with two back-to-back tasks that the student is easily able to complete. Then, when you give the difficult task, the student is already engaging in a pattern of following instructions.

Context

This strategy can be used across different settings and for a wide variety of tasks. Use prior to giving a difficult demand like starting homework, turning off electronics, doing a chore, or during transitions.

Tip

When choosing easy tasks to give, make them related to the target task.

For example, if the target task is to start working on homework, first you could say "bring me backpack" (easy task), "sit down at table" (easy task). When you are ready to give the target task, the student has already started the task.

No compliance

By initially presenting a difficult task, the student may feel overwhelmed, resulting in noncompliance.

First easy task

Start with a simple task that the student can easily complete.

Hard task

Build on the momentum by presenting the difficult task immediately following compliance of the easy tasks.

Compliance

The student will be more likely to comply to the difficult task after experiencing success with completing the previous tasks.

Second easy task

Continue by immediately giving another easy task to complete.

Providing Choices

Increasing compliance

Goal

By providing choices, the student will be more likely to cooperate, be motivated to work and stay engaged in the task

How

When possible, provide choices related to the task and provide choices of rewards to earn. By allowing the student to feel that he has control over the environment, he will be more motivated to participate.

Context

Types of task-related choices may include:

- Order of tasks (e.g. reading or writing homework first)
- Materials to use (e.g. crayons or markers)
- Person to work with (e.g. Mom or Dad)
- Choosing where to sit (e.g. student's desk or small table)

Tip

When offering choices for rewards, the teacher can ask, "Do you want to work for ____ or ____?").

For visual learners, the teacher may provide a visual of reward options from which the student can choose (see "Tools," pg. 136).

Choice of demand

Provide choice

The teacher provides a task-related choice: a choice of which task to complete first. The teacher could have also provided a choice of which toothbrushes to use.

Choice of reward

Provide choice

Prior to giving the task demand (math test), the teacher provides choices of rewards that the student can earn. This allows the student to choose an item that will motivate him to work.

Student makes choice

When the student is able to make their own choice, they have more control over the task which often leads to more motivation.

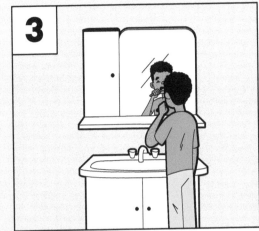

Compliance

The student is successful with completing the tasks in the order that he chose.

Student makes choice

The student has chosen a reward that is motivating for him. It may be helpful to keep this reward, or a picture of the reward, close by as a reminder for what he is working to earn.

Compliance

The student is successful with completing the task and earned the reward that he chose.

Reactive Strategies

Introduction

While proactive strategies are often used on an ongoing basis to prevent problematic behavior from occurring, reactive strategies are used once the behavior has already occurred. These are called consequences (or reactions) to the behavior.

While many people associate the word 'consequence' with something aversive, in ABA, 'consequence' means whatever happens after the behavior. The consequence can be reinforcing (meaning the student is more likely to do the behavior again in the future) or punishing (meaning the student is less likely to do the behavior again the future). As many times we are the ones providing the consequence; thus, we can choose how to react to influence whether that behavior occurs again.

Consequences

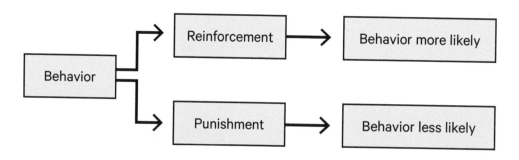

Reactive strategies aim to minimize reinforcement for problematic behavior and to maximize reinforcement for desirable behavior. While punishment is an effective reactive strategy, research shows that by increasing focus on reinforcing desired behaviors, students will learn to engage in these appropriate behaviors instead.

Goals
- Increase positive behaviors
- Reduce problematic behaviors

Things to consider
- Does the student like to receive praise, attention?
- Does the student prefer receiving attention from adults or peers?
- What items/activities are most reinforcing to the student?
- Does the student engage in problematic behaviors to escape from tasks?
- How often does the student need reinforcement?
- Is the student able to work for a delayed reward?
- Is the student able to track his own progress towards a goal?
- What is a desired replacement behavior?

How to Use
- Determine if you want to increase or decrease a specific behavior
- Choose a strategy
- Adjust the strategy to match the student's skill level and specific behaviors

Strategies to increase positive behaviors
- Behavior contract
- Token economy
- Teaching better behaviors

Strategies to decrease problematic behaviors
- Extinction
- Blocking Aggressive Behaviors
- Managing Repetitive Behaviors

Tell, Show, Do

Three steps to increase compliance

Goal

Increase student compliance with non-preferred tasks & decrease the amount of teacher repeated demands

How

Consistently use the steps (tell, show, do) to follow through with the demand. Reinforce when compliance occurs.

Tip

Place this visual strategy where the challenging target task usually occurs as a self-reminder for how to complete the steps (e.g. hang on student's bedroom wall if 'get dressed' is a challenging task).

Context

This is an effective strategy for a variety of challenging demands. Use these steps during times when the student is not following directions.

Remember that when you give an instruction but don't follow through, the student is learning it's ok to ignore that instruction. Be prepared to always follow through!

Tip

When giving an instruction, use a statement rather than asking the student to complete the task.

Example

Don't say, "can you take off your shoes?" as the student might respond, "no." Instead, say, "take off your shoes."

1

Trace the triangle!

Tell

Give the verbal instruction for the task and wait five seconds for the student to start.

Do

Physically guide the student to complete the task, removing the assistance when possible. Do not provide reinforcement, instead, move on to the next task instruction.

Show

Give the instruction again along with a gesture towards the task (pointing) <u>or</u> modeling the task (show student how to do it). Wait five seconds for response.

Reinforce

As soon as the student starts the task, give praise. When she has competed the entire task, give a bigger reward (e.g. excited praise, a favorite toy, or a break).

Reinforce

As soon as the student starts the task, give praise. When the task is completed, give a bigger reward.

Token Economy

Creating clear expectations and clear rewards

Goal

Token economies help students visualize progress towards a goal and learn to work for a delayed reward

How

Identify the skills/behaviors (max five) that you want to promote. Then, determine what items or activities can be earned. Create rules for how tokens can be earned and when they can be cashed in for the reward. Make adjustments over time as needed (i.e. increase the amount of tokens needed to earn).

Context

Token economies are commonly used in schools and home settings. The rules of the token economy are customizable for the student's/teacher's needs.

Try using

- To increase completing household chores
- To complete assignments at school
- To refrain from a problematic behavior for a certain period of time
- To increase social interactions with peers

Tip

- Ask for the student's input on rewards available to earn. This will increase the motivation to work for them!
- Try making a customized token board with the student's favorite characters as faces instead of stars.

Set up

Determine the rules for the token system and teach them to the student.

Earning tokens

Add a token to the token board for each completed task or occurrence of a target behavior.

Introduce

Remind the student what task needs to be completed in order to earn a token, as well as what reward he is working to earn.

Follow through

Provide praise for task initiation and for completing the target task.

Earning rewards

Once the student fills the token board with tokens, he earns the reward.

Reward

Give the reward as soon as the token board is full. The token board will be cleared and ready to use again.

Teaching Better Behaviors

Replacing a problematic behavior with a better behavior

Goal

Reduce problematic behaviors and teach a more appropriate, alternative behavior.

How

Identify why a problematic behavior is occurring and then teach the student a better, more appropriate, way to get their needs met. Only reinforce this appropriate behavior and ignore or redirect the problematic behavior.

Context

After determining the appropriate behavior you want to see increase, reinforce (e.g. give praise, attention, etc.) every time the student does this behavior. Over time and after multiple successes, reduce the number of times you are giving the reinforcement.

Tip

For problematic behaviors that occur because the student wants a specific item, like a toy or favorite food (function: access), the replacement behavior could be appropriately asking for the item (see "Teaching to Request," pg. 106).

For problematic behaviors that occur because the student does not want to complete a task (function: escape), the replacement behavior could be asking for a delay in starting the task or earning a break after part of the task is complete.

Identify the target and the function of behavior

Here, the student is calling out to get the teacher's attention.

Teach a replacement behavior

Teach the student a more appropriate way to get what they want.

Here, the teacher is showing the student that if he wants the teacher's attention, he should raise his hand instead of yelling out.

Amount of Reinforcement

The more independently the student is engaging in the better behavior, the more reinforcement he should receive. Here the teacher is providing extra attention by coming to the students desk to call on him. Here the teacher is providing extra attention by coming to the student's desk to call on him.

Reinforce the better behavior

Every time the student engages in better behavior, immediately give reinforcement (here, the teacher is providing attention by calling on the student). If the student engages in problematic behavior, move back to step 2. Remind them of what behavior they should do.

Reinforce others

Provide reinforcement (here, giving attention) to other students who are engaging in the better behavior. Ignore the problematic behavior. This will give a hint to the student of what he should do to get what he wants (here, attention).

Extinction by Function

Access and attention

Goal

Effectively reduce problematic behavior

How

Determine what the reinforcer is for a behavior, then withhold that reinforcer.

To identify what the reinforcer is, collect ABC data (see pg. 30) for at least four instances of the target behavior. Look for patterns to determine the function (reason the behavior is occurring). More information on page 33.

Context

Once the function is identified, use extinction across all settings and people. The more consistent extinction is, the better the success with reducing the problematic behavior.

Tip

If a problem behavior is more severe (e.g. aggression, self-injurious behavior, etc), you can do planned ignoring by:

- Physically blocking the behavior using as minimal physical contact as necessary
- Keeping your face neutral
- Avoiding eye contact
- Refraining from talking to the student

Problematic Behavior

An example of a problematic behavior (student throwing objects) across each function.

Function **access**

Learned behavior

The student has learned through experience that engaging in the problem behavior leads to accessing a preferred item.

Use extinction

Following the problematic behavior, do not allow the student to access the desired item.

Function **attention**
(planned ignoring)

Learned behavior

The student has learned through experience that engaging in the problematic behavior leads to getting attention from others. Remember that reprimands (e.g. "No," "Don't do that," "Stop") are also forms of attention.

Use extinction

Following the problematic behavior, do not provide any attention to the student. Avoid eye contact and keep your face neutral.

Extinction by Function

Escape and sensory

Goal

Effectively reduce problematic behavior

How

Determine what the reinforcer is for a behavior, then withhold that reinforcer.

To identify what the reinforcer is, collect ABC data (see pg. 30) for at least four instances of the target behavior. Look for patterns to determine the function (reason the behavior is occurring). More information on page 33.

Context

Once the function is identified, use extinction across all settings and people. The more consistent extinction is, the better the success with reducing the problematic behavior.

Tip

When the function is escape, use Tell, Show, Do strategy (pg. 68) to follow through with the demand.

Problematic behavior

An example of a problematic behavior (student throwing objects) across each function.

Function **escape**

Learned behavior

The student has learned through experience that engaging in the problematic behavior leads to escaping a non-preferred task.

Use extinction

Following the problematic behavior, do not allow the student to escape completing the work task. Continue to represent the task and follow through.

Function **sensory**

Learned behavior

The student has learned through experience that engaging in the problematic behavior leads to a pleasing feeling or sensation.

Use extinction

Identify ways to alter the environment or materials to not allow the student to experience the pleasing feeling following a problematic behavior.

Blocking Problematic Behavior

Blocking and redirecting
to a better behavior

Goal

Teacher will block problematic behavior from occurring
and will redirect the student to the appropriate
replacement behavior

How

When a student attempts a problematic behavior, the
teacher will first block the behavior, then immediately
redirect the student to the appropriate behavior.

It is important that the teacher first understand why
the problematic behavior is occurring so they can
redirect to the appropriate behavior (see "Functions of
Behavior," pg. 33).

Context

Use this strategy following student engagement or
attempt at problematic behavior.

Example

A student engages in pica (eating nonedible items).
The student begins to eat play-doh. The teacher blocks
by removing play-doh from student's mouth and putting
her fingers in front of the mouth. The teacher redirects and
shows the student how to build a snowman out of play-doh.

Tip

For most aggressive behaviors, you can block by using
your forearm and open palm. You also may need to
clear the area of items that may be thrown as a way of
blocking throwing,

Problem behavior

The student approaches the teacher and
attempts a problematic behavior.

Note: The teacher is already aware why
this student engages in hitting. Here, the
function is to get attention.

Block

The teacher blocks the problematic behavior.

Redirect

The teacher redirects the student to a more appropriate behavior.

Here, the teacher is modeling how to tap on her shoulder in order to get attention. The teacher is turned away from the student (not giving attention), until the student does the better behavior (tapping on the shoulder).

Reinforce appropriate behavior

Once the student has engaged in the appropriate behavior, the teacher will provide reinforcement.

Here, the student is tapping on the teacher's shoulder to request attention. This is appropriate, so the teacher turns and gives attention.

Official title: Response Interruption and Redirection

Managing Repetitive Behaviors

Decreasing vocal and physical repetitive behaviors

Goal

Over time, decrease engagement in vocal and physical repetitive behaviors (e.g. scripting, repeating vocal sounds, hand flapping, body rocking)

How

When a repetitive behavior occurs, immediately interrupt the behavior and redirect the student to another behavior.

Context

This strategy can be used anytime repetitive behavior is occurring. Although this strategy manages the behavior after it is occurring, it should reduce the occurrence of the behavior over time.

Tip

Vary the types of interruption and redirection you use to continue the student's compliance.

Vocal

Repetitive vocal sounds

Follow these steps immediately upon hearing the vocal repetitive sounds.

Physical

Physical repetitive movements

Follow these steps immediately upon seeing the physical repetitive movements.

Interrupt

Interrupt, or block, the behavior. For vocal noises, interrupt by talking over the student.

Redirect

Redirect the student to engage in a behavior that cannot be done at the same time as the repetitive behavior. For vocal, have the child answer a question or copy a sound that you make.

Interrupt

Interrupt, or block, the behavior. For physical movements, interrupt by initiating a different movement.

Redirect

Redirect the student to engage in a behavior that cannot be done at the same time as the repetitive behavior. For physical movements, try high fives, wiggling arms, spinning body, or clenching fists.

Teaching New Skills

Introduction

Many parents and teachers share a common goal of wanting to assist their students in learning new skills and becoming more independent. This may include increasing independence in self-care tasks, improving expressive communication skills, learning social and play skills or even building academic skills. The skills that you want to teach the student may change over time, however, the strategies in this chapter can be used across situations and ages. It is important to recognize that students may acquire skills at different rates, and even further, a student may learn some skills more quickly than other skills. With continued practice and patience, you can help the student make meaningful changes in his life.

There are a variety of effective strategies as well as various teaching styles, so it is important to consider how the student learns best. In ABA, skill acquisition goals are typically customized to meet the student's specific needs. Answer the questions listed below ('Things to consider') to determine how to create a reasonable goal for your student and how to best help them achieve this goal.

Goals
- Build independence
- Improve current skills
- Teach new skills

Things to consider
- What is the student's current skill level relating to this target skill?
- What is a reasonable goal for the student based on their skill level?
- Does the student learn better from watching or doing?
- Does the student learn better from visual or verbal instructions?
- Who else can practice this skill with the student?
- What are other ways we can practice this skill?

How to use
- Determine what type of skill you want to teach
- Choose a strategy
- Adjust the strategy to match the student's skill level

Strategies to increase communication skills
- Teaching new requests

Strategies to increase independence
- Task analysis
- Problem solving

Strategies to increase social skills
- Pairing
- Joint attention
- Play skills

Strategies to use when teaching any type of skill
- Shaping
- Modeling
- Naturalistic teaching
- Generalization

Pairing

Building relationships
to increase success

Goal

Build compliance with adult instruction and improve
social interactions with peers

How

By making connections with yourself and preferred
items/activities, the student will associate your
presence with the fun experience. This will make the
student more likely to follow your instructions, and with
peers, be more likely to engage in social interactions.

Context

Pairing is important when establishing a relationship
with a new person; like a new teacher or a new friend.
Parents can practice pairing to improve already
established relationships.

Tip

A good way to pair yourself as 'fun' is to offer toys and
activities that the student only has access to with you
and cannot access himself. Another way to increase
pairing is to offer help with the student's preferred
activities, such as helping a student build a train track.

To build compliance

Identifying preferences

Place several items/activities out for the
student and watch to see which he
chooses.

To improve social skills

Identifying preferences

Place several items/activities out for the
student and watch to see which he
chooses.

Play with no demands

Join in on the activity that he chose and play without giving any demands (including 'play demands' like "push it this way" or "go faster"). Follow the student's lead!

Assist in pairing peer

Give another student an item that could help with the activity that the main student has chosen.

Assist in peer play

By having a peer take new items to the preferred play activity with the student, the student will be more likely to have a positive reaction to that peer and may start socializing.

Naturalistic Teaching

Finding teaching moments

Goal

Teach skills in the student's naturally occurring routines and daily activities to encourage learning in natural contexts

How

Look for ways to increase learning opportunities in the student's typical day.

Consider the skills the student is currently learning and create ways to practice these skills in naturally occurring contexts. For example, if a student is learning colors and is currently playing with Legos, the teacher may suggest, "let's build a blue tower!"

Context

Teaching should occur during typical daily activities or routines. The teacher can create more opportunities by laying out materials that could promote learning.

Tip

Follow the student's lead! Observe what interests the student and think, "how can I turn this into a learning moment?"

Skill I want to teach

_____

_____

_____

_____

_____

_____

Naturalistic ways I can teach this skill

_____

_____

_____

_____

_____

_____

_____

_____

_____

_____

_____

_____

_____

_____

_____

_____

_____

_____

_____

_____

_____

_____

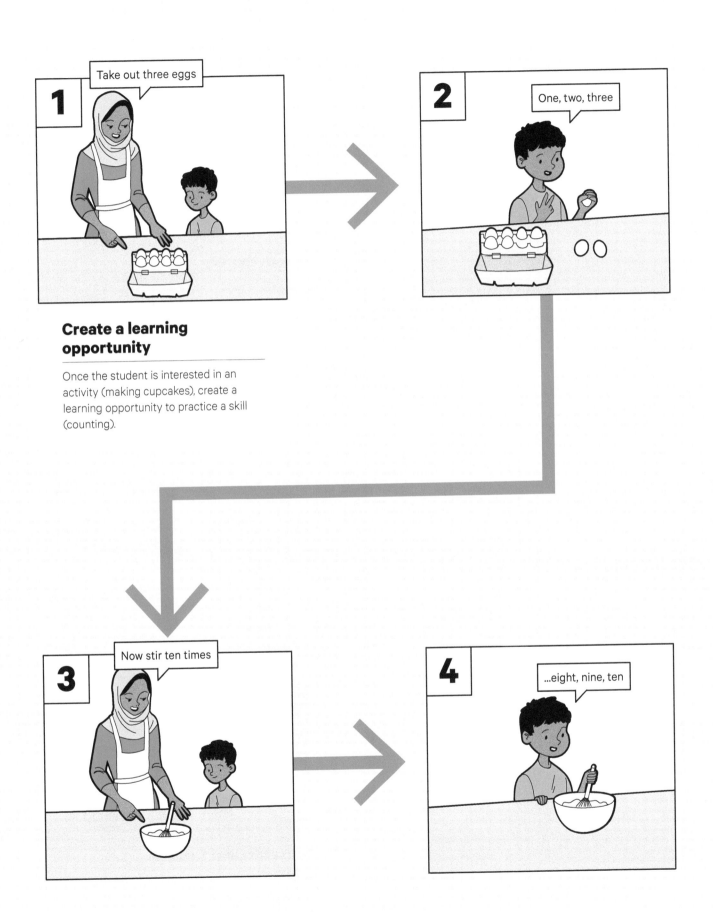

Create a learning opportunity

Once the student is interested in an activity (making cupcakes), create a learning opportunity to practice a skill (counting).

Breaking Down Skills

Teaching a new, complex skill

Goal

Teach a new, complex skill by breaking it down into a sequence of smaller steps

How

The teacher will develop the task analysis (TA) by writing down the small steps necessary to complete the task/activity.

The teacher will systematically teach each step, one at a time, providing assistance as needed.

Context

Task analysis are often used to teach adaptive skills such as washing hands, brushing teeth, getting dressed, tying shoes, doing chores, making a meal and crossing the street. Create a task analysis for any complex skill that can be broken down into simple steps.

Tip

Remember to practice the steps yourself after you have created the TA to ensure that they are in correct sequence and nothing was left out. Often visuals are a great way to assist in learning the skill sequence (see "Tools" pg. 142). Try to reduce teacher assistance and increase student independence each time the skill is practiced.

Create the TA

Teacher will write down the steps needed to complete the task. Each step should be one simple action.

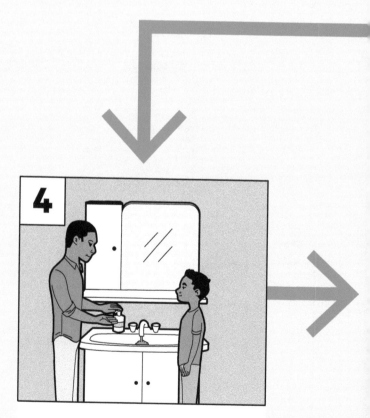

Assist student through steps: model

This father is using a "model prompt," in which he is showing the student how to do the next step.

Assist student through steps: gesture

If the student needs assistance, provide a "prompt" or reminder of what to do. This father is pointing to the faucet to remind the student to turn on water.

Now rinse your hands

Assist student through steps: verbal

This father is providing a "verbal prompt" by verbally telling the student what the next step is.

Nice scrubbing!

Reinforce independence

For any step that the student can already do independently, provide praise (and refrain from prompting).

Great job rinsing your hands!

Reinforce learning

Provide specific phrase (stating exactly what was done well) anytime the student completes a step indepedently for the first time.

Problem Solving I

Teaching independence
in finding solutions

Goal

Student will independently recognize a problem,
generate possible solutions, choose a solution and
evaluate its effectiveness

How

Guide the student through each step in the problem
solving process while emphasizing their collaboration
and eventual independence.

Context

Use these steps each time a new problem arises.
The process is the same whether it is a small problem
(e.g. running out of notebook paper) or a bigger
problem (e.g. being bullied at school).

Problem

Student encounters a problem.

Choose

Encourage the student to choose one
solution and try it.

Identify

First, ask the student to identify what the problem is.

Options

Together with the student, name as many solution options as possible, good or bad.

Evaluate

Evaluate whether the solution worked or if there's a need to try a different solution.

Conclusion

If the chosen solution solved the problem, the goal is reached. If not, return to step 4.

Problem Solving II

Teaching independence in finding solutions

Identify problem

The student identifies what the exact problem is. Here, the student is missing an item needed to complete the task.

Goal

Increase independence in finding solutions to novel problems

How

Teach a structure for what to do when encountering a new problem. The student will learn to come up with and try solutions until the problem is solved.

Context

These steps can be used across a variety of problems: missing items, broken items, item is out of reach, a task is too difficult, etc.

Tip

The teacher may need to initially assist the student through these steps by helping provide solution suggestions or reminding them to try another solution. With practice, the student should move through the steps independently.

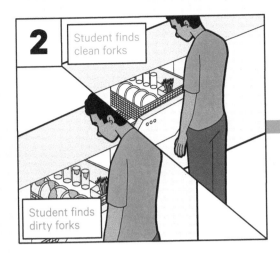

Try solution 1

The student should think of and try the first solution. If this works, they can complete the task. If it doesn't work, move on to the next step.

Try solution 2

The student should think of and try another solution. If this works, they can complete the task. If it doesn't work, they continue trying new solutions.

Problem Solved

The student was able to find a successful solution and can now complete the task.

Shaping & Fading

Teaching a new skill over time

Goal

Shaping: Teach a target new skill
Fading: Increase independence over time

How

Reinforce the student's progress in coming closer and closer to the actual target skill. This can be done over time (as in the first visual example) or during one sitting with repeated tries (as in the second visual example).

To shape a skill, start by teaching a small part of the skill and continue to build the skill with practice.
In fading, start by providing full support then fade out your assistance over time.

Context

Shaping is frequently used when teaching expressive communication (e.g. teaching a student to speak), but can be used with a wide variety of skills.

Fading is often used when teaching adaptive skills starting with full teacher assistance and then gradually letting the student become more independent.

Shaping language

Starting to learn

Reinforce any initiation in a new skill. For expressive communication, this could be making the first sound of the word.

Here, the reinforcement for all attempts of saying "cookie" will be giving the cookie to the student.

Fading to build independence in skill

Starting to learn

Reinforce any initiation in a new skill. For adaptive skills, you may need to start with full assistance. Here, the reinforcement can be giving praise, or giving access to a favorite item after the student has practiced the new skill.

Improving

Reinforce progress. Once the student has improved on the skill, only reinforce that level of the skill (e.g. do not give a cookie if he only says "kuh").

Independent

Once the student has mastered the skill, only reinforce that level of the skill (i.e. only give the cookie if he says "cookie").

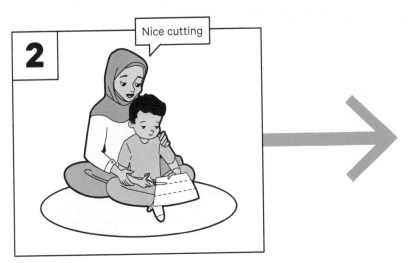

Improving

Reinforce progress. As the student is improving, slowly remove your assistance, which will increase their independence.

Independent

Fade your assistance until the student is independently doing the skill.

Modeling

Teaching by showing

Goal

By showing how to do a skill, the student may be able to learn the skill by copying the actions

How

Act out a specific skill that you would like the student to learn (called "modeling" the skill). The student may independently begin to imitate you, or you might give the instruction "your turn" or "now you try" to encourage them to imitate the same skill.

Context

Modeling is often used in everyday life as a way for individuals to learn new skills. Individuals often learn social skills and self-help skills by watching others' actions. Promote learning new skills by following the modeling steps.

Tip

Video modeling has also shown to be an effective learning strategy, especially in teaching social skills and play skills. The student watches a video of someone acting out the skill, then will imitate the skill on their own.

Modeling
Social skills

Model

Act out the target skill in a situation in which this skill would likely be used.

Here, the teachers are modeling conversation skills while eating dinner.

Modeling
Self-help skills

Model

Act out the target skill using materials that are likely to be used.

Here, the teacher is modeling how to hold the pencil and write the student's name.

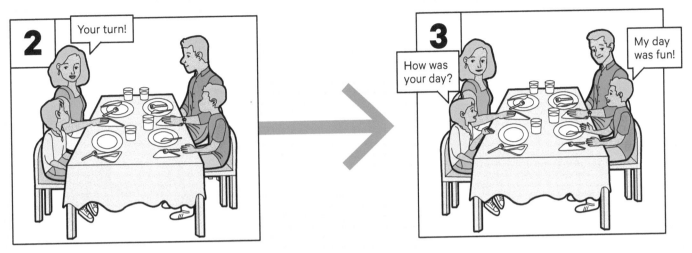

Request

Immediately following the model, ask the student to imitate the skill.

Feedback

Provide feedback on what was done well and what could be improved for next time.

Request

Immediately following the model, ask the student to imitate the skill.

Feedback

Provide feedback on what was done well and what could be improved for next time.

Generalization

Expanding learning

Goal

Expand learning of one skill in a particular setting (e.g. tying shoes at home) to being able to apply that skill in various settings (e.g. school, park) and in various ways (e.g. different shoes). This is called "generalization."

The goal is that the skill will emerge in situations that haven't been specifically taught.

How

When teaching a new skill, consider different locations, people, and materials that could be introduced to expand the learning of this skill.

Context

All skills must be generalized in order to say that a student has "mastered" that skill.

Teach and practice the skill in a variety of contexts until the student can do the skill in novel contexts. For example: teach the student to answer "what's your name?" with parent, teacher, and sibling. If a peer asks the student, "what's your name?" and the student correctly answers, this skill is likely mastered!

Tip

For some students, first, teach a new skill in a structured setting prior to practicing it in a variety of contexts. For other students, you can teach in a variety of contexts from the beginning. Think about how your student learns best!

Teach the skill

- With various people
- In various settings
- With various materials
- Using varied language
- At various times of the day

Play Skills

Teaching play skills to improve social relationships

Goal

Assist the student with progressing through play skill development in order to build their social relationships

How

- Determine where the student is currently on the states of play skill development
- Set the goal as the type of play that is the next stage
- Practice this play type with the student by modeling what to do and making play related comments (e.g. "I'm a pirate!")
- Reinforce the student's attempts at copying your actions or comments.

Context

When teaching play skills, it is helpful to practice the skills with the student a few times before moving to playing with peers.

When the student is ready to practice with peers, the teacher can initially assist by modeling what to do, then gradually pull back to let the students play alone.

1. Onlooker

The student is watching peers play, but is not interacting with them or the play materials.

4. Pretend play

The student is using items in creative ways to pretend they are something else or that he is someone else.

2. Parallel Play

The student is playing alongside peers and may or may not be completing the same activity. However, they are not engaging with peers.

3. Associative play

The student is playing with the same materials as a peer and may talk to or look at the peer, but they are not working together to complete the activity.

6. Cooperative play

The students play a game or an activity together and share a common goal. They use social skills to take turns and talk about the activity.

5. Social play

The student learns social play skills including sharing and taking turns. The student may request for items from the peer.

Joint Attention

The start of social skills: Teaching to share a common interest

Goal

Teach the student to follow, initiate, and join in on social interactions by sharing a common interest.
Joint attention also helps students learn to use others' facial expressions and gestures as sources of information.

How

Use shaping strategies (see pg. 96) to teach two main types of joint attention: responding to joint attention and initiating joint attention. Practice with different toys, activities, and people (adults and peers).

Context

Teach and refine these skills in natural and play settings. Create games that will target building joint attention skills. Example: hide toys and teach the student to follow your point, head turn, or eye gaze in order to find them.

Tip

Use exaggerated verbal and facial expressions while interacting with a toy to help the student learn to use others' faces as a cue for what they are thinking. Example: a block tower falls over. Make an exaggerated "surprise" face by raising your eyebrows, covering your mouth, saying "uh-oh!". If the student looks at you, reward them with "good looking!" or giving a quick tickle, etc.

With teacher

Responding

Use a preferred toy to gain the attention of the student. Move the toy around and encourage the student to follow it with her eye gaze. Pass the toy across your face to promote eye contact during play.

Initiating

Reinforce any initiations of joint attention from the student. If the student points to something, look at it and respond positively. Example: "Oh, you see a dog! It's so cute!"

With peers

Responding with peers

Set the student up for success with their peers by providing preferred toys that the students can attend to together. You may need to assist in responding to peers by saying something like, "look she has a doll!"

Initiating with peers

Place preferred items/activities between peers to encourage them to play and interact together. You may need to assist in initiating joint attention and sustaining the attention.

Prior skills needed

Student
- Being able to request needs
- Being able to copy others

Teacher
- Paired as a reinforcer (student should have experience with the teacher being fun/having fun activities)

Teaching to Request

Teaching how to ask
for wants/needs

Goal

- Reduce a problem behavior by teaching the student a replacement, and more appropriate, way of getting their needs met
- Build communication skills

How

Teach the student exactly what to say to request their needs appropriately. Depending on the student, this could be a one-word request ("cookie"), a multi-word request ("I want cookie"), the use of sign language or picture exchange (PECS). Withhold the desired item/attention until there is a correct response. Repeat cycle for increased effectiveness.

Context

Use this strategy anytime the student has motivation to request something: a toy, food, attention, help with a task, etc. This motivation may look like the student reaching towards something they want or engaging in problematic behaviors.

Tip

Try using a visual prompt of a sentence starter (see "Tools," pg. 144) as a visual reminder for what the student should say.

Remember to require the student to use appropriate requests across all people and settings.

Identify motivation

Identify what the student has a motivation to request for: an item, attention, help, etc.

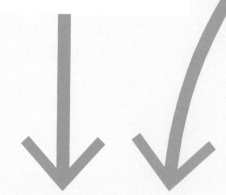

Question

First, give the student the opportunity to identify what he/she wants/needs.

Correction

Directly correct the student by saying the correct response, then return to step 2 and re-ask the question.

Reinforcement

Give the student what they have appropriately asked for. This could be: an item, attention, help, etc.

Response

The student responds, either by correctly naming what they want or by engaging in problematic behavior.

Putting it all Together

Introduction

The following chapter is intended to be used once you feel confident in your understanding of the previous chapters. Here, you will learn how to use multiple strategies to tackle some of the more challenging life moments. The common challenges chosen were based on years of professional experience as well as through a poll of parents. For each common challenge, a suggested package of strategies is provided. These strategies include the proactive and reactive strategies featured in detail earlier in the book. The page numbers for each strategy are provided in case you need to reference them for further understanding.

In ABA, this strategy package is often called a Behavior Intervention Plan (BIP). This refers to the steps that teachers should consistently do in order to manage this specific challenge. For the fastest and most effective results, it is recommended that once you determine the steps you will use, you are consistent with following them. Further, it is helpful if all caregivers follow the same steps so that the student learns what to expect.

You may have found that some strategies are more effective or relatable with your student. Unlike the other chapters where following the steps in the sequence is crucial, here, the strategies are arranged as a guideline. You can adjust the steps as needed to best fit your needs. For example, if 'Priming' is not effective on its own with your student, there is no need to include it as part of the entire strategy package. You may choose to leave it out or replace it with a strategy that works better for your student, perhaps 'First, Then.' This chapter is all about what works best for you!

Turning off Electronics

Goal

Teach the student how to follow through with the demand of turning off electronics (e.g. Ipad, phone, video games, computer)

How

- Teachers will use a variety of strategies to build compliance with the demand.
- Teachers must use extinction (following through with the demand) in order to reduce problematic behaviors.

Context

Use these strategies prior to giving the instruction of turning off electronics to reduce the likelihood of problematic behaviors.

Tip

When asking to turn off electronics, try telling the student to "turn off and put down" rather than "turn off and give to me." For some students, it's easier if they can control where they put it, rather than having to give it to someone else.

Priming (pg. 56)

Prior to giving the demand to turn off, give a transition warning. You can say, "five more minutes on (device)." It may help to give a one minute warning as well.

Show me your score!

Easy, easy, hard (pg. 60)

Use the 'easy, easy, hard' strategy to build compliance prior to giving the difficult 'turn off' demand. First, give two easier demands relating to the electronic game (e.g. "show me your score!," "tell your friends 'bye'").

Extinction (pg. 74)

Follow through with demand and do not allow the student to continue accessing the item after you have given the instruction to turn it off. Use Tell, Show, Do strategy to follow through.

Reinforcement (pg. 40)

If the student complies with the demand, give social praise ("nice job listening!"). Also, it is ideal if the student can earn electronics again later as a reward for complying with the instruction.

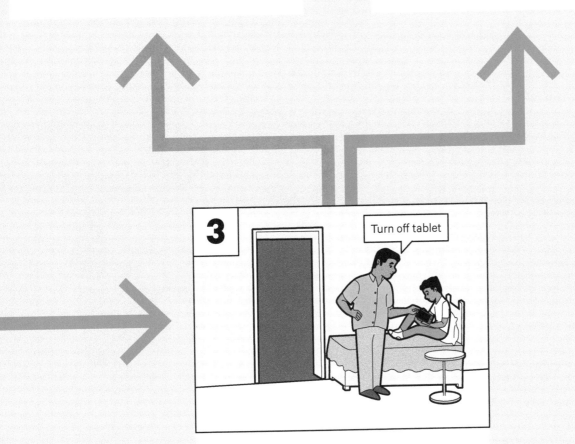

Tell, show, do (pg. 68)

Use Tell, Show, Do strategy to give a clear instruction ("turn off (device)") and follow through with that demand.

Here, the teacher is doing the 2nd step of gesturing to the off button.

Staying on task

Goal

Increase the amount of time student is on task and the amount of work that is completed. Teach the student to complete tasks in order to earn breaks from the task.

How

- Teachers will use a variety of strategies to build compliance with a demand task.
- Teachers must use extinction (following through with the demand) in order to reduce problematic behaviors.

Context

Use these strategies during times when there are problematic behaviors relating to avoiding a demand task (e.g. completing homework, completing an assignment at school).

Priming (pg. 56)

Prior to giving the demand, give a transition warning. This can be in the form of "five more minutes with (preferred item)" or "five more minutes until we do (task)."

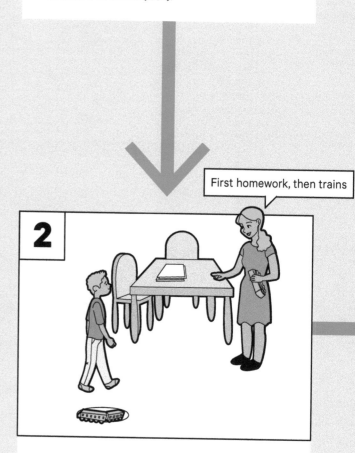

First, then (pg. 58)

Use "First, Then" language to remind the student what he is working for. You may also hold the reward in sight. "First (task), then (reward)."

Extinction (pg. 74)

If the student attempts to avoid the task, follow through with the demand that was given and do not allow the student to escape completing the task. Use Tell, Show, Do strategy to follow through (page x).

Reinforcement (pg. 40)

Provide breaks from the task only following periods of compliance. Try giving short breaks after each page of completed work and a longer break after completing the entire task.

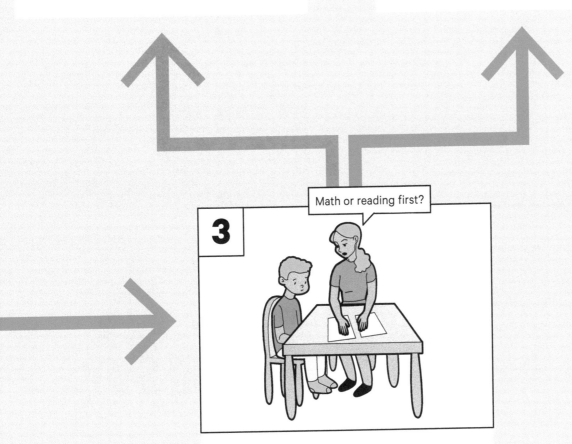

Math or reading first?

Provide choice (of demand) (pg. 62)

Provide a choice relating to the demand tasks.
Try offering a choice between:
- Doing front or back of worksheet first
- Doing math or reading task first
- Using crayons or colored pencils
- Using blue or black pen
- Having Teacher 1 or Teacher 2 assist

Classroom Disruptions

Goal

- Reduce classroom disruptions that are caused by students trying to get attention
- Teach students appropriate ways to gain peer and teacher attention

How

- Teachers will use a variety of strategies to help students learn how to request/earn attention appropriately.
- Teachers must use extinction (not providing attention) in order to reduce disruptive behaviors.

Context

Use these strategies with one target student or across all students to prevent and reduce disruptive behaviors in the classroom.

Priming (pg. 56)

Prior to transitioning from a free period to a work period, teacher will inform students of the expectations for the upcoming activity (e.g. sitting quietly at desk, raising hand to ask/answer questions).

Be proactive

Give attention (e.g. calling on them to answer, giving praise) to the target student(s) at predictable and frequent rates. Gradually increase the time between giving attention. By giving attention at frequent rates, the student will be less likely to act out in order to try and get attention.

Extinction (pg. 74)

Ignore the disruptive behaviors. Turn body/face away from the student to minimize attention. For highly disruptive behaviors, minimally block and redirect to appropriate behavior (model raising hand).

Reinforcement (pg. 40)

Immediately following initiation of appropriate behavior (raising hand), reinforce by providing attention (calling on student). Following several instances of appropriate behavior, provide additional attention (having student come to front of class).

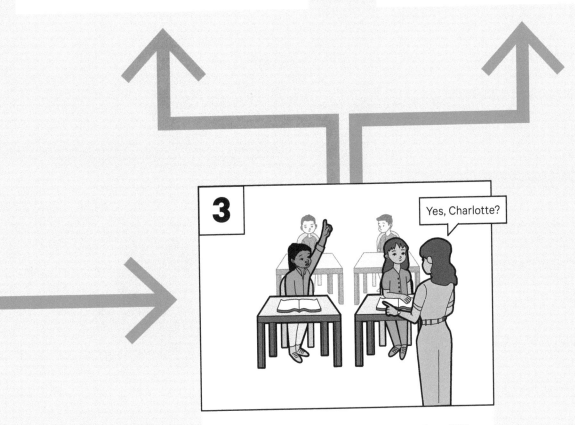

Yes, Charlotte?

Teaching better behaviors (pg. 72)

Provide reinforcement (giving attention) to the student only following the better way to request attention (e.g. raising hand). Provide attention to other students who are engaging in appropriate behaviors as a signal of what is expected.

Sharing Toys

Goal

Increase tolerance in waiting for a turn with preferred items and improve social/play skills

How

- Set clear expectations for sharing
- Model how to appropriately wait for a turn
- After a few successful times sharing, gradually increase the amount of time the student needs to wait for the item.

Context

Practice these steps during play times when the student and another person are both interested in playing with the same item. These steps can also be practiced as a role play where the teacher says, "let's practice sharing!" and pretends to be a peer who is interested in the item.

1

Remember, two minutes then switch

Priming (pg. 56)

Remind students of expectations while sharing preferred items (e.g. each person gets x amount of minutes, then switch).

2

Modeling (pg. 98)

Model appropriate behavior while waiting for turn: sitting calmly, watching other person, not reaching for item.

Extinction (pg. 74)

Block attempts the student makes to access the item when it's not their turn.

Reinforcement (pg. 40)

If the student independently gives up the item when their turn is over, provide praise or other reinforcement.

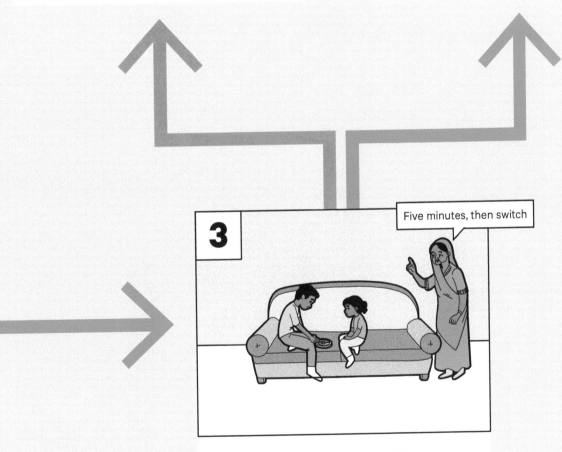

Shaping (wait time) (pg. 96)

As the student practices this skill, gradually increase the amount of time they need to wait for the item.

Accepting "No" or "Wait"

Goal

Teach the student how to accept and tolerate denied access (being told "no") and how to wait for preferred items/activities

How

- Use a variety of strategies to teach the student when they can have access (visual schedule), how to appropriately request the item or more time with the item (requesting needs), or how to redirect self to another item (providing choices).
- Teachers must use extinction (following through with the denied access) in order to reduce problematic behaviors.

Context

Use these strategies during times when there are problematic behaviors relating to denied access (e.g. student requested an item/activity and was told "no," student requested more time with an item/activity and was told "no").

1

Priming (pg. 56)

Create a visual schedule depicting when preferred items/activities will be available during the day

2

Providing Choices (pg. 62)

When a preferred item/activity is not available, provide at least two alternative choices that are moderately or highly preferred items/activities.

Extinction (pg. 74)

When the student is engaging in problematic behaviors, teachers will ensure that the item remains removed and/or denied. You may need to prompt the student to remind them how to appropriately request/wait for items/activities.

Reinforcement (pg. 40)

Following appropriate behaviors (tolerating "no," appropriately requesting needs, waiting for preferred item), the student will earn reinforcement. Use shaping to gradually increase the amount of time the student needs to wait in order to receive the reinforcement.

Requesting needs (pg. 106)

When the student engages in appropriate behaviors to request for an item/activity, praise will be given. If possible, access to the item/activity will also be given.

Picky Eating

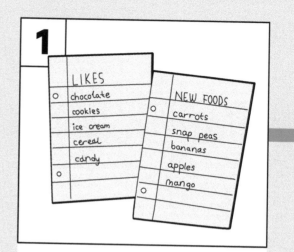

Identify foods

Create a list of foods that the student currently likes to eat (these will be the rewards). Create a list of new foods to try.

Goal

Increase student's acceptance of new foods (primary focus should be on fruits and vegetables)

How

Use First, Then strategy for each bite of food:
"First (new food), then (favorite food)."

Over time, increase the amount of bites of the new food the student is expected to eat in order to have the favorite food.

Context

Create a list of foods that you would like the student to learn to accept. Consider what food groups they are currently not eating enough of. Consult a doctor for specific dietary recommendations. Practice this strategy at snack time every day. Once the student is comfortable eating five bites of a new food before receiving the favorite food, start adding this new food to their usual meal times (e.g. pack it in their lunchbox, serve it with breakfast, etc.).

Note

If the student does not accept the bite of the new food, say "that's ok, but no (favorite food)" and take away all food. Try again once the student requests for the favorite food again. *The favorite food must only be given following the student eating the new food.*

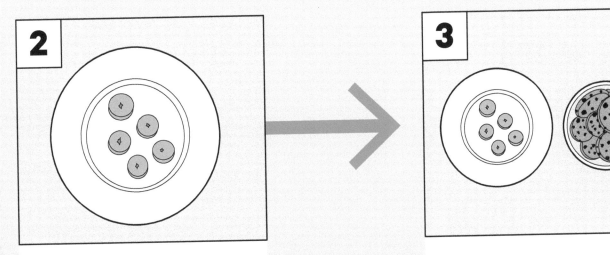

Cut in small pieces

Cut the new food into five small pieces. You may need to start very small (size of an M&M) before gradually getting bigger in bite size.

Set up

Place five small bites of new food next to a large amount of the favorite food.

One bite of new food

Give the instruction, "First (new food), then (favorite food)."

One bite of reward

For each bite of new food the student eats, she can have one bite of the favorite food. Continue for at least five bites.

Following Directions

Goal

Increase student compliance and decrease the amount of time it takes to complete a task

How

By giving clear instructions, following through with the demand given, and reinforcing efforts, the student will be more likely to follow the direction.

With consistent use of these steps, the student will begin to have better compliance overall.

Context

These steps can be used for any instruction but should be used consistently with difficult instructions.

Tip

Place this strategy in settings where the student typically has trouble following directions (e.g. in their bedroom, at their desk, in the car, etc). This will help you remember to use the steps during challenging times.

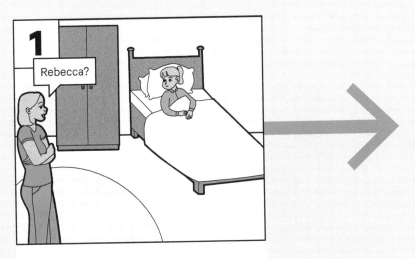

Gain attention

Before giving an instruction, make sure to gain student's attention (eye contact)

Clear, short, instruction

Give the instruction using a short and clear phrase. Do not phrase in a question form ("Can you...?")

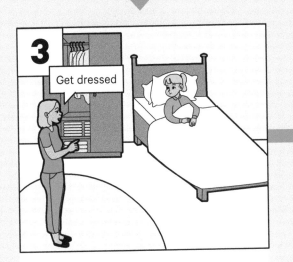

Follow through (pg. 68)

Use Tell, Show, Do strategy to follow through with the instruction.
First tell the student what to do, then show them what to do, then physically assist them in completing the task.

Reinforce (pg. 40)

Give praise once the student starts the task. When the student completes the task, give a bigger reward.

Transitions

Goal

Increase compliance during transitions from highly preferred activities to non-preferred activities

How

Prepare in advance by informing the student about the upcoming change. Use a combination of compliance building strategies to assist with the challenging task of transitioning.

Context

Use these steps when there is an expectation for the student to transition from a highly preferred task (e.g. recess, free play at home, watching TV, playing on electronics, playing with friends) to a less-preferred task (e.g. classwork/homework, chores, going somewhere in the car).

Prime 1 (pg. 56)

Prior to a transition that may be challenging for the student, give a 'prime' of what change is upcoming.

Prime 2 (pg. 56)

Just before the instruction to transition activities, give one more reminder about what is upcoming (and the upcoming expectation).

Easy, easy, hard (pg. 60)

Start the transition with an easy demand relating to the activity (here the teacher is saying to do a 'big jump!'). Immediately follow this with another easy demand ("stand behind me"), finally, give the challenging demand (here, going inside).

Follow through (pg. 68)

If at any point in giving the 'easy, easy, hard' demands, the student does not follow the instruction, move into the 'Tell, Show, Do' strategy to follow through with the demand.

Reinforcement (pg. 40)

After the challenging transition is complete, make sure to give reinforcement.

Learning Personal Information

Goal

Assist the student in learning important personal information: name, age, birthday, address, phone number, parents' names

How

Use a variety of strategies that are effective ways to teach new skills. Adjust the strategies to fit the student's skill level and practice through repetition.

Context

It is important for individuals to know their personal information as a safety precaution.

Learning this information may require substantial teaching effort and repetition, but the use of these strategies will help the student learn and remember the information more quickly.

Naturalistic teaching (pg. 88)

Find natural opportunities to practice answering the questions. The more practice, the better.

Shaping (pg. 96)

Start small and build the student's answer over time. This is especially relevant for longer answers like phone numbers and addresses. Teach just a few numbers at a time.

Modeling (pg. 98)

Show the student how to answer the question correctly, either through verbally saying the answer or writing the answer down (whichever way the student learns better).

Generalization (pg. 100)

Once the student is making progress with answering the question, have other people ask the question. This will ensure the student can still answer correctly when a new person asks.

Learning to Talk

Goal

Increase expressive communication skills (e.g. language sounds and words)

How

Use a variety of strategies that are effective ways to teach new skills. Adjust the strategies to fit the student's skill level and practice through repetition.

Context

A common feature of individuals with Autism is having a delay in language/speech. Here are some indicators that the student is more likely to begin talking:

- makes babbling noises when playing
- imitates sounds
- watches people's mouths when they are speaking
- makes singing sounds
- makes babble labels for items, although the babble may not sound similar to the item's name
- has some receptive language skills (understanding what others are saying- as shown by looking when their name is said or following simple instructions)

Reinforcement (pg. 40)

Use the strategies of effective reinforcement to reward the student's attempts at talking and give big rewards when they say their first sounds/words.

Shaping (pg. 96)

Start by first teaching the student to mimic sounds. Listen for sounds that they are already starting to make while babbling.

Modeling (pg. 98)

Gain the student's attention and then model (using enunciated mouth movements and sounds) the word or sound that you are teaching.

Generalization (pg. 100)

Practice the skill with a variety of people to promote learning.

Naturalistic teaching (pg. 88)

Use the student's motivation to guide which words you teach. Many students' first words are items that they want (e.g. favorite toy, favorite food).

Tools

Introduction

The following pages contain templates, tools, and resources to assist you in teaching your student. The intention is that you may copy, cut out, and use the tools provided alongside the strategies you learned in this book. You can also find these tools online on our website.

Visual supports

Visual supports are a means of communicating through pictures or text instead of using words. Visual supports convey a lot of information in a manner that is easy for students with language delays to understand. However, they are not just helpful for students with language delays. We all use similar kinds of visual supports in our day-to-day lives because sometimes a visual representation of information is the best way for us to process information. We rely upon street signs to tell us where to go, calendars to keep track of appointments, and lists at the grocery store. Each of these strategies is a kind of visual support.

Visual supports can help students learn new skills, know what is expected of them, and improve self-management skills. Through visuals, teachers can better communicate with students, as students can learn to better communicate with their peers and teachers. With consistent use, visual supports can also promote independence and reduce problematic behaviors.

Research indicates that visual supports help by:
- Allowing students to focus
- Making abstract concepts more visually concrete
- Allowing students to express their thoughts
- Providing routine and structure
- Reducing anxiety
- Serving as a tool to assist with transitions

Visual supports for students with Autism:

Some individuals with Autism find it difficult to understand and follow verbal instructions. They may have challenges sufficiently expressing what they want or need. Visuals can help teachers communicate what they expect. This decreases frustration and may help decrease problem behaviors that result from difficulty communicating. Visuals can promote appropriate, positive ways to communicate.

For individuals who experience anxiety relating to changes in routines or when they are in unfamiliar situations, visuals can help them understand what to expect and will happen next in order to reduce anxiety.

Token Board

Goal

Increase compliance and motivation to complete target tasks

How

Provide reinforcement in form of praise and token for each completed task, then provide a larger reinforcer when all tokens have been earned.

Context

- Use as a visual reminder of what can be earned for completing the target tasks
- Use to build compliance with a variety of tasks
- Use to teach delayed reinforcement (earning something rewarding later)
- Use to teach self-management (student can learn to give himself tokens after completing tasks)

Instructions

1. Copy this page and cut out all pieces
2. If possible, laminate pieces for longer use
3. Ask student to choose reward to work for
4. Place reward icon on token board
5. Place a star token on each blank square as the student completes tasks
6. When the board is full with the six stars, the student earns the reward

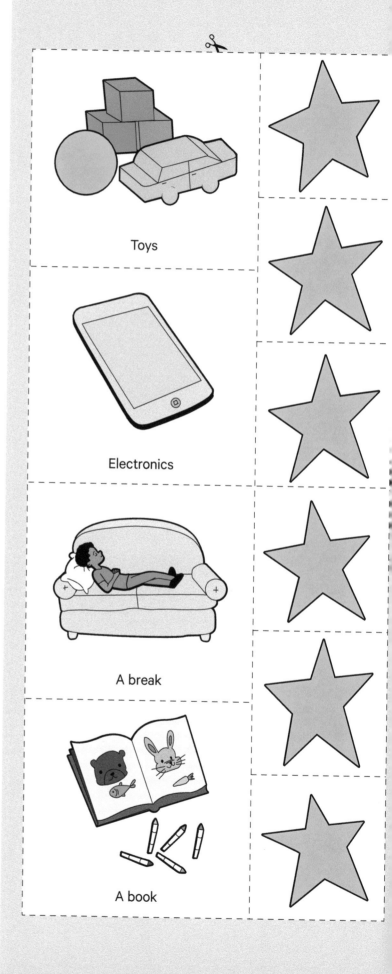

Toys

Electronics

A break

A book

I am working for

Place reward icon here

Place first
star here

Behavior Contract

Goal

Promote responsibility and self-regulation, improve student motivation and effort, provide structure and consistency

How

Involve the student in setting up the expectations and choosing rewards to earn. Initially guide the student in building independence by reminding them to review the contract and determine if they are meeting goals.

Context

Behavior contracts can be used at home and in school settings; some students may have one contract for home expectations and one contract for school expectations.

Use with students who exhibit persistent behavior problems, challenges with organizational skills or challenges with completing daily tasks.

Instructions

1. Copy this page and cut out contract template
2. Determine the target behavior to improve
3. Work as a team (teacher, parent, student) to create the rules for the contract- what is expected and what can be earned
4. Everyone agrees and signs
5. Promote independence by having the student review the contract daily/weekly to determine if they earned the reward

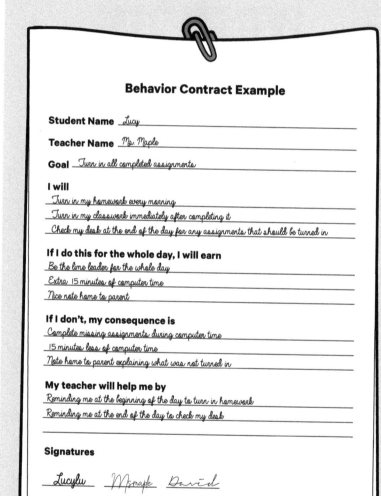

Behavior Contract Example

Student Name _Lucy_

Teacher Name _Ms. Maple_

Goal _Turn in all completed assignments_

I will
Turn in my homework every morning
Turn in my classwork immediately after completing it
Check my desk at the end of the day for any assignments that should be turned in

If I do this for the whole day, I will earn
Be the line leader for the whole day
Extra 15 minutes of computer time
Nice note home to parent

If I don't, my consequence is
Complete missing assignments during computer time
15 minutes less of computer time
Note home to parent explaining what was not turned in

My teacher will help me by
Reminding me at the beginning of the day to turn in homework
Reminding me at the end of the day to check my desk

Signatures

Lucylu   _Msmaple_   _David_

Student Name _____

Teacher Name _____

Goal _____

I will

_____

_____

_____

If I do this for the whole day, I will earn

_____

_____

_____

If I don't, my consequence is

_____

_____

_____

My teacher will help me by

_____

_____

_____

Signatures

_____   _____   _____

Visual Schedules

Goal

Improve compliance during typical routines and transitions between tasks. Reduce problem behaviors related to changes in schedules.

How

Provide predictability and structure by outlining the tasks/activities that will be completed that day. Reinforce independence in completing these tasks and transitioning between the activities.

Context

A daily schedule can be created for certain time periods such as a morning routine, after school routine, or bedtime routine. In a classroom, the daily schedule could be posted for the entire day, or split into morning and afternoon schedules.

Tip

Include preferred activities on the schedule to break up the non-preferred tasks and keep motivation high.

Instructions

1. Cut out all pieces and if possible, laminate for longer use.
2. Place picture icons on schedule in order that the events should occur. You can make a schedule for the entire day, or just for the morning or bedtime routine.
3. You can move pictures from the left column to the right column as they are completed, or if you fill all the blocks with activities, remove the icons as they are finished.

Daily schedule ✁ _____ routine

Task Analysis

Goal

Teach a new, complex skill by breaking it down into a sequence of smaller steps

How

Use the visuals created as a step-by-step guide to increase independence in completing each of these everyday activities.

Context

Place the task analysis in the setting it will be used (e.g. 'brushing teeth' in the bathroom). Point to the steps to assist the student in moving through them. After several practices, the teacher will stop pointing and the student will use the pictures as the guide.

Instructions

1. Copy this page, cut out each Task Analysis, and laminate if possible for longer use.
2. Place the Task Analysis in the area where that skill takes place.
3. Initially, guide the students through the steps by pointing to each step as it should occur. Teacher may need to provide other types of prompts (see Breaking Skills Down, pg. 90).
4. As the student becomes more independent in the skill, they will follow the visual steps on their own, without a teacher present.
5. When the student has mastered the skill, remove the Task Analysis.

Washing hands

Brushing teeth

Getting dressed

   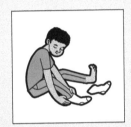 

Crossing the street

Buttoning shirt

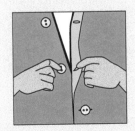 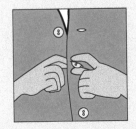 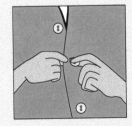

Sentence Starter Card

Goal

Improve expressive communication skills to better request needs

How

Use proactively
Use these sentence starter cards as a visual reminder for the student to ask appropriately for wants/needs (instead of engaging in problematic behavior).

Use to manage problematic behavior
When the student starts to engage in a problematic behavior because he wants something, show one of these cards and only give the item once the student says the sentence in a calm voice.

Context

These sentence cards should be used with students who are able to say 3-5 word sentences.

For students who are currently making one-word requests (e.g. "play-doh"), try starting with the "I want ____" card to build language to three-word requests.

Instructions

1. Make a copy of this page
2. Cut out sentence starter strips and if possible, laminate for longer use
3. Use along with the Teaching to Request strategy, pg. 106

I want to play with _____

I want _____

Can I play _____

Can I have _____

First, Then Visual

Goal

Increase compliance and motivation in completing tasks

How

When giving an instruction, remind the student what they will earn afterward by using text, pictures, or verbal reminder in "first, then" terms.

Context

Use this visual with students who respond better to visuals rather than verbal instructions. You can also use this visual along with the verbal instruction and continue to point to the visual as a reminder for what the student needs to do.

Instructions

1. Identify a reward that will likely be motivating for the student.
2. Write or add pictures on the "First" and "Then" boxes. The "First" box should contain the task the student should complete. The "Then" box should contain the reward that the student will earn.
3. Use this visual along with the verbal instruction, "First (target task), then (reward)" (pg. 58).

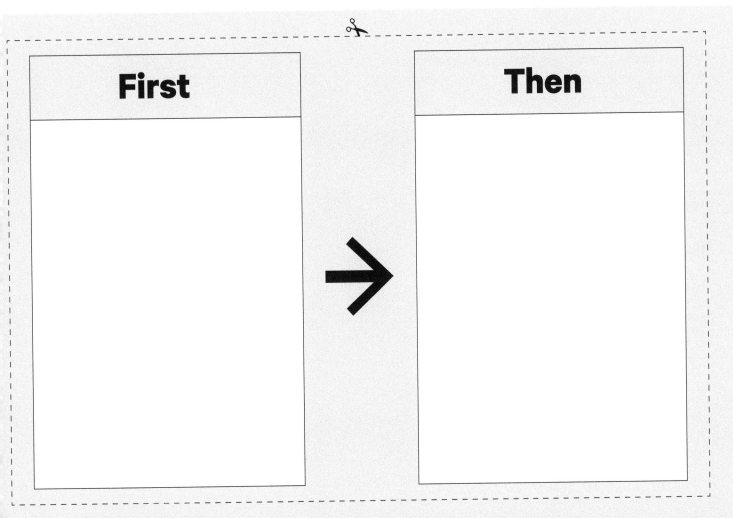

ABC Data Collection Sheet

Goal

Determine the reason the problem behavior is occurring by looking for clues happening before and after the behavior

How

When a new problematic behavior is occurring, write notes describing the situation surrounding each occurrence of the behavior in order to find clues that suggest why the behavior is occurring.

Context

Collect ABC Data for each problematic behavior that is currently occurring. Additionally, anytime new problematic behaviors arise, the first step is to collect ABC Data.

Instructions

1. Collect ABC Data (see how, pg. 30) for at least four times the problematic behavior occurs.
2. Use the information you collected to determine the likely function of the behavior (see how, pg. 33).

Student name _____

Date _____

Time	Setting & People Present

Antecedent	Behavior	Consequence	Function
What happened before the behavior?	Describe the behavior	What happened after the behavior?	

Resources

Recommended Products

Sensory Products
- Munchables: Chewelrey, Fidgets
- Noise Reduction Headphones
- Transformer Sensory Sack
- Classroom Break Box
- Strechy Sensory Fidget Strings
- Massage Roller
- Exercise bands (put on chairs)
- Liquid Floor Tile

Picky Eating Products
- 8 the Plate

Fine Motor Skills
- Let's go Finger Fishing
- Shape Sorter
- String a Farm Beads
- Mighty Mind
- I Can Tie My Shoes!
- Count and Sort Stacking Tower
- Dimpl
- Skoolzy Peg Board Set

Social Skills
- Social Inferences Fun Deck
- Photo Feelings Fun Deck
- 204 Fold & Say Social Skills

Toys/Games
- Friends and Neighbors: The Helping Game
- Cat in the Hat I Can Do That! Game
- Dinosaur Escape Game
- Social Skills: 6 Board Games in 1
- ThinkFun Roll and Play Game

Behavior Management Products
- Ring Alarm Contact Sensor
- MotivAider
- Wet Stop
- OK to Wake! Alarm Clock and Night-Light
- Vagreez 30 and 5 Minute Sand Timer

For the Classroom
- Stickerpop.com / Stickerpop! App
- Time Timer
- Adjustable Seating: Kore Wobble Chair, Hokki Stool, Seating Disc, Stability Ball
- EZ Stick Classroom Line-Up Helpers
- Desk Privacy Shields
- E.Z.C. Reader Strips

Books
- Behaviorspeak: A Glossary of Terms in ABA By Bobby Newman
- Would you Teach a Fish to Climb a Tree? By: Anne Maxwell
- More than Words By Fern Sussman
- What Shamu Taught Me About Life, Love, and Marriage By Amy Sutherland
- The Verbal Behavior Approach By Mary Barbera
- How Are You Feeling Today? By Molly Potter
- Poke a Dot Book Series (10 Little Monkeys, Goodnight Animals,
- Old MacDonald's Farm, Who's in the Ocean?, etc) By Melissa & Doug

References

American Psychiatric Association. (2013). Diagnostic and Statistical Manual of Mental Disorders (5th ed.). Washington, DC.

Baker, Jed (2008). No More Meltdowns – Positive Strategies for Managing and Preventing Out-of-Control Behavior. Arlington, TX: Future Horizons, Inc.

Boesch, M.C., Taber-Doughty, T., Wendt, O., Smalts, S.S. (2015). Using a behavioral approach to decrease self-injurious behavior in an adolescent with severe autism: a case study. Education and Treatment of Children, 38(3), 305-328.

Boutot, A., & Hume, K. (2012). Beyond time out and table time: Today's Applied Behavior Analysis for students with autism. Education and Training in Autism and Developmental Disabilities, 47, 23-38.

Bryce, C. I., & Jahromi, L. B. (2013). Brief report: compliance and noncompliance to parental control strategies in children with high-functioning autism and their typical peers. Journal of Autism and Developmental Disorders, 43(1), 236+.

Buron, Kari Dunn, & Curtis, Mitzi (2003). The Incredible 5-Point Scale. Shawnee Mission, KS: Autism Asperger Publishing Company.

Carr, E.G. & Durand, V.M. (1985). Reducing problem behaviors through functional communication training. Journal of Applied Behavior Analysis, 18(2), 111-126.

Conroy, M. A., Asmus, J. M., Boyd, B. A., Ladwig, C. N., & Sellers, J. A. (2007). Antecedent classroom factors and disruptive behaviors of children with autism spectrum disorders. Journal of Early Intervention, 30(1), 19-35.

Cooper, J.O., Heron, T.E., & Heward, W.L. (2007). Applied behavior analysis (2nd ed.). Upper Saddle River, NJ: Pearson Education, Inc.

Cooper, J.O., Heron, T.E., & Heward, W.L. (2019). Applied behavior analysis (3rd ed.). Upper Saddle River, NJ: Pearson Education, Inc.

De Bruin, C., Deppeler, J., Moore, D., & Diamond, N. (2013). Public School-Based Interventions for Adolescents and Young Adults With an Autism Spectrum Disorder: A Meta-Analysis. Review of Educational Research, 83(4), 521-550.

Durand, V.M. & Carr, E.G. (1991). Functional communication training to reduce challenging behavior: maintenance and application in new settings. Journal of Applied Behavior Analysis, 24(2), 251-264.

Durand, V.M. & Moskowitz, L. (2015). Functional communication training: thirty years of treating challenging behavior. Topics in Early Childhood Special Education, 35(20),116-126.

Eckenrode, L., Fennell, P., & Hearsey, K. (2004). Tasks Galore for the Real World. Raleigh, NC: Tasks Galore.

Eldevik S., Hastings R. P., Hughes J. C., Jahr E., Eikeseth S., Cross S. Meta-analysis of early intensive behavioral intervention for children with autism. Journal of Clinical Child & Adolescent Psychology. 2009

Falcomata, T.S., Muething, C.S., Gainey, S., Hoffman, K., Fragale, C. (2013). Further evaluations of functional communication training and chained schedules of reinforcement to treat multiple functions of challenging behavior. Behavior Modification, 37(6), 723-746.

Gerhardt, P.F., Weiss, M.J., Delmolino, L. (2004). Treatment of severe aggression in an adolescent with autism: non-contingent reinforcement and functional communication training. The Behavior Analyst Today, 4(4), 386-394.

Hart Barnett, J. (2018). Three Evidence-Based Strategies that Support Social Skills and Play Among Young Children with Autism Spectrum Disorders. Early Childhood Education Journal., 46(6), 665–672.

Harvey, Shane T et al. (2009). Updating a Meta-Analysis of Intervention Research with Challenging Behaviour: Treatment Validity and Standards of Practice. Journal of Intellectual & Developmental Disability, 34(1), 67–80.

Lovaas, I., Newsom, C., & Hickman, C. (1987). Self-stimulatory behavior and perceptual reinforcement. Journal of Applied Behavior Analysis, 20(1), 45–68. http://doi.org/10.1901/jaba.1987.20-45

Maag, John W. (2001). Powerful Struggles: Managing Resistance, Building Rapport. Longmont, CO: Sopris West Educational Services.

Mancil, G.R. & Boman, M. (2010). Functional communication training in the classroom: a guide for success. Preventing School Failure, 54(4), 238-246.

Martínez-Pedraza, F. de L., & Carter, A. S. (2009). Autism Spectrum Disorders in Young Children. Child and Adolescent Psychiatric Clinics of North America, 18(3), 645–663. http://doi.org/10.1016/j.chc.2009.02.002

Moes, D.R., Frea, W.D. (2002) Contextualized behavioral support in early intervention for children with autism and their families. J Autism Dev Disord, 32(6), 519-33.

Moyes, Rebecca A. (2002). Addressing the Challenging Behavior of Children with High-Functioning Autism/Asperger Syndrome in the Classroom. Philadelphis, PA: Jessica Kingsley Publishers.

Myles, Brenda Smith, & Southwick, Jack (2005). Asperger Syndrome and Difficult Moments: Practical Solutions for Tantrums, Rage, and Meltdowns. Shawnee Mission, KS: Autism Asperger Publishing Co.

Raulston, T., Hansen, S., Machalicek, W., McIntyre, L., & Carnett, A. (2019). Interventions for Repetitive Behavior in Young Children with Autism: A Survey of Behavioral Practices. Journal of Autism and Developmental Disorders., 49(8), 3047–3059.

Rao, Shaila M., Gagie, Brenda. (2006). Learning through Seeing and Doing: Visual Supports for Children with Autism. Teaching Exceptional Children, 38(6), 26-33.

Rispoli, M., Camargo, S., Machalicek, W., Lang, R., Sigafoos, J. (2014). Functional communication training in the treatment of problem behavior maintained by access to rituals. Journal of Applied Behavioral Analysis, 47, 580-593.

Stichter, J. P., Randolph, J. K., Kay, D., & Gage, N. (2009). The use of structural analysis to develop antecedent-based interventions for students with autism. Journal of Autism and Developmental Disorders, 39(6), 883-96.

Wacker, D.P., Schieltz, K.M., Berg, W.K, Harding, J.W., Dalmau, Y.C.P., Lee, J.F. (2017). The long-term effects of functional communication training conducted in young children's home settings. Education and Treatment of Children, 40(1), 43-56.

Wagner, Sheila (1998). Inclusive Programming For Elementary Students With Autism. Arlington, TX: Future Horizons, Inc.

Index

CPSIA information can be obtained
at www.ICGtesting.com
Printed in the USA
LVHW050633051119
636240LV00005B/226/P